All of Us Are Present

All of Us Are Present

The Stephens College Symposium
Women's Education: The Future

Edited by Eleanor M. Bender,
Bobbie Burk, and Nancy Walker

 James Madison Wood Research Institute
Columbia, Missouri, 1984

Copyright © 1984 James Madison Wood Research Institute
for the Study of Women's Education
Stephens College, Columbia, Missouri 65215
Library of Congress Catalog Card Number 83-081649
ISBN 0-916767-01-9
Printed and bound in the United States of America
All rights reserved

Permission to quote sections of "When I Was Growing Up,"
by Nellie Wong, from *This Bridge Called My Back: Writings
by Radical Women of Color*, granted by Persephone Press.

**For Betty Littleton
and Bernice Williamson**

Preface

As part of a celebration of its 150th anniversary, Stephens College held a symposium, *Women's Education: The Future*, on February 15–18, 1983. The speeches and discussions revolved around the progress of women's education during the time since the founding of the college, but more importantly, the place women's education should take in the future, how educators of women can best serve their constituency. Patricia Albjerg Graham, Dean of the Harvard Graduate School of Education, and the Charles Warren Professor of the History of Education at Harvard University, gave the keynote speech. Gerda Lerner, the Robinson-Edwards Professor of History at the University of Wisconsin, spoke on the first topic, the effect of societal change on the lives of women. Patricia Bell Scott, an Assistant Equal Opportunity Officer at the Massachusetts Institute of Technology, talked about the educational needs of women of varying ages and backgrounds. Elizabeth Kamarck Minnich, a member of the faculty of the Union for Experimenting Colleges and Universities, addressed the role of the college curriculum in preparing women for the challenges of the future. Bernice Resnick Sandler, an Executive Associate with the Association of American Colleges and the Director of the Project on the Status and Education of Women, spoke on the fourth topic, the preparation of women to become agents of change in society. These essays are the essence of those speeches with appropriate modifications for publication. Members of the Stephens College faculty have written summary reports of the panel discussions that followed each speech. The order of the essays and summaries is that of the Symposium itself. The final synthesis session moderated by Sheila Tobias, Professor of Political Science at the University of Arizona, is summarized here by Bobbie Burk.

Special thanks and appreciation are due the campus Planning Committee, the National Advisory Board, and the administration and Board of Curators of Stephens College.

A complete listing of everyone directly involved with the symposium is included in the appendix.

This is the first publication of the James Madison Wood Research Institute for the Study of Women's Education, affiliated with Stephens College. The Wood Institute Board of Directors wishes to thank Susan McGregor Denny for her consultation in preparing the texts for publication, Ed King for his design of this book, and Dave Hoffmaster, who took the photographs.

EMB
December 23, 1983

Contents

Nancy Walker
Introduction, *1*

Patricia Albjerg Graham
The Cult of True Womanhood: Past and Present, *9*

Gerda Lerner
The Rise of Feminist Consciousness, *33*

Nancy Walker
The Effects of Social Change on the Lives of Women: Summary Session 1, *51*

Patricia Bell Scott
Education for Self-Empowerment: A Priority for Women of Color, *55*

Bernice Williamson
Special Needs of Women: Summary, Session 2, *67*

Elizabeth Kamarck Minnich
From Fate to Inheritance, *71*

Jeanine L. Elliott
The Curriculum: Summary, Session 3, *87*

Bernice Resnick Sandler
Educating Women for Change: How to Grow "Movers" and "Shakers," *91*

Kathy H. Reese
Women as Agents for Change: Summary, Session 4, *109*

Bobbie Burk
Synthesis Session, *115*

Bobbie Burk
Afterword, *121*

Appendix I: Workshops, *123*
Appendix II: The Speakers and Panelists, *127*
Appendix III: Symposium Planning Committee, *131*
Appendix IV: Participants, *133*
Bibliography, *137*   Index, *141*

Nancy Walker

Introduction

All of Us Are Present is both celebration and invitation. In its 150th year, Stephens College invited educators from across the country to participate in a symposium, "Women's Education: The Future." Those of us who organized the symposium were aware of the great changes in women's lives and educational needs during the years that this college and others have existed; we wished to honor a heritage of change and innovation in meeting those needs. Yet we also felt a sense of urgency about the future of education for women in a period characterized by changing social roles, rapid technological advancements, and new insights into the ways women learn and develop. For three days in February of 1983, several hundred people—faculty members, students, and administrators representing sixty colleges and universities and twelve professional associations—listened to speakers and panel discussions, asked questions, and met in workshop groups to challenge each other and the educational community to develop new ways of thinking about the education of women.

What becomes clear in the texts of the major speeches and the summaries of panel discussions is that women's education affects and is affected by concerns that reach far beyond the classroom environment. This symbiosis must become apparent to all of us who educate women today. As I talk with women students at all age levels, in classrooms and over coffee, I sense both their energy and their confusion. The media predict their brilliant futures in occupations newly open to them or yet to be invented, but problems of sexism

Sheila Tobias, moderator of the final session, talks with a symposium participant.

and racism persist. They are feminists in belief, but sometimes reject the term, and most have little sense of the history of women's struggle for those freedoms they enjoy. The ambivalence that Patricia Graham speaks of in her keynote address to the symposium is both a valid assessment of women's attitudes toward their own futures and a challenge to all who are involved in their education. Just as the educational experience shapes the values and expectations of women students, and therefore determines in large part the impact these women will have on government, business, the arts, and the economy, so the method and substance of education is the result of societal realities: the structure and values of a culture and its institutions, the relationship between private decisions and public policies. If there is a central thesis in *All of Us Are Present*, it is that education has been shaped by the forces of male-dominated history, technology, biology, and systems of belief, while largely ignoring the contributions, achievements, and experiences of over half the world's population: women. All of are indeed present in the creation of generations of women students who will both inherit and redirect those forces.

The Stephens symposium is provocative rather than prescriptive. By focusing on four central themes and inviting speakers, panelists, and participants to move these themes into a vision of the future, the symposium asks for a re-vision of education for women, not just the revision of courses and programs. Participants urge working for educational change from the bottom up rather than making patchwork alterations, and begin with the assumptions of our institutions themselves, which, as Elizabeth Minnich points out in "From Fate to Inheritance," embody "a set of discrepancies worked into our tradition so thoroughly that we are all caught by them." The issues are therefore fundamental and holistic, rather than specific or partial, and represent a new beginning for educators. Efforts to forecast the future accurately force us to speculate and dream, and to revert time and again to history, which assures us that change is right and that women's role in change is their right.

In 1983, the number of people who devoted their professional lives to the education of women specifically—as teachers, scholars, administrators—was encouragingly large. A list of the symposium speakers and their positions testifies to the increasing influence women have on higher education, and the diversity of their backgrounds and interests contributes to the richness and complexity in this volume. Selection of the themes, speakers, and panelists for the symposium was the result of collaborative effort—itself a consistent thread in this book—on the part of many people. The four basic emphases in *All of Us Are Present* are the effects of social change on women's lives, the diversity (in age, in racial and ethnic background, in economic level) of women students, the structure and content of the college curriculum, and the necessity to make women agents rather than recipients of change. Yet none of these is entirely separable from the others, as Patricia Graham suggests in the keynote address. Stressing the interrelatedness of education and society, Graham states that "the higher educational institutions in this country have played a unique role in forming women's conceptions of themselves and in mediating society's expectations for women."

The speakers represented in this volume share some important assumptions. One of these is that to some extent women's lives and experiences are and will remain different from those of men in certain fundamental ways. As Minnich points out in "From Fate to Inheritance," the term "*man* simply does not, in fact, include everyone"; therefore, the tradition that women inherit often does not even include them. Patricia Bell Scott extends this sense of separation to point out its double effect on women of color, set apart by both gender and race. Including in her term "women of color" blacks, Hispanics, Asians, and Native Americans, Bell Scott stresses the diversity of their backgrounds and needs but points to the common truth that "the prevailing attitude about our education has been that we are only capable of (and should be trained for) work without intellectual challenge and work which enhances our moral character." Women of color, like all women, are being "educated away from themselves" by a system based on white male traditions and values. Yet woman's assumed and actual "difference" involves us finally in the paradox that women's biological difference, while on the one hand a souce of discrimination and exclusion, is at the same time the source of a nurturant quality, which, as Gerda Lerner points out, should be valued in both sexes because of its potential for human survival.

A second shared assumption is that women should know their own heritage as women. Graham's speech, reviewing the attributes of "true womanhood" at various points in American history, typifies the kind of knowledge women should have about the effect of cultural values on self-definition; and the major thesis of Lerner's "The Rise of Feminist Consciousness" is that an awareness of their own tradition frees individual women from "struggling against the weight of tradition . . . in isolation" and enables them to build upon the work of others instead of having to reinvent the wheel. Arguing that "women's history is woman's right," Lerner asserts that such study "validates women's experience as a basis from which to generalize and create social theory." Minnich calls for a revision of both language and conceptualization as fundamental to a redefinition of tradition, and says that the task of those undertaking a "feminist critique of the liberal arts tradition" is to "bring wholeness and diversity to a partial, singular tradition." The new scholarship on women, viewed by all the symposium speakers as an essential ingredient of curricular change, is for Minnich only the beginning of a revolution in thinking that would regard the received tradition as partial, incomplete, and therefore false. Bernice Sandler, in "Educating Women for Change: How to Grow 'Movers' and 'Shakers,'" sounds the same note and provides an example of language distorting reality when she points out that students who are told that American women were "given" the vote in 1920 will assume that women were passive recipients of this right rather than the shapers of their own destinies. And Patricia Bell Scott's insistence on our recognition of diversity in women's backgrounds and cultural values in "Education for Self-Empowerment: A Priority for Women of Color" suggests the complexity and challenge of presenting women's heritage as a revision of tradition in all parts of the curriculum.

As the term *self-empowerment* in Bell Scott's title suggests, a further point of agreement among the speakers is that education must equip women to determine the direction of their own lives, and, further, to influence the lives of humankind. Sandler addresses this point directly in "Educating Women for Change," but symposium speakers and participants repeatedly referred to this function of education. The submissiveness that Graham identifies as one prescribed characteristic of the mid-nineteenth-century woman may have given way to the ambitiousness of the women of the 1980s, but education must play a far greater role in preparing women to be involved in change rather than merely responding or adjusting to it, according to Sandler. Pointing out that the socialization of girls and women still encourages passivity instead of power, she first explores some factors of this socialization and then suggests ways in which colleges and universities may involve women in "the politics of change." Gerda Lerner's definition of feminism as involving both autonomy and self-definition provides an ideological framework for these suggestions, especially when self-definition includes "the authority to define one's ideas about the world and the universe." Minnich's insistence that we redefine what is "human"—to include, for example, "natality" as well as "mortality"—becomes part of the empowering theme when viewed in the light of Lerner's emphasis on knowledge as prerequisite to social change.

A fourth basic assumption underlying the dialogue in these pages is that education can and does make a difference in women's lives—that, in fact, *only* education has the power to counteract and ultimately alter the lives and values of both women and men in significant ways, and that education at all levels must consciously seek this goal. The effectiveness of college education in bringing about change is due partly to a certain kind of elitism: college-level study, as Sandler points out, is requisite for most prestigious and therefore influential positions, and one half of the ten million people attending college in 1980—and thus potentially occupying these positions—were women. More fundamental is the fact that the college experience, both inside and outside the classroom, affects the very process of thought. As Minnich puts it, "Our feelings are named for us by great thinkers and writers and scholars, by psychologists, philosophers, historians, poets. If they are not named for us, they become, as [Hannah] Arendt put it, our fate." If the "great thinkers" to which women students are exposed represent only a white male tradition and mode of thought, women's nature and experience are not validated and women are not empowered. Women's colleges, Sandler feels, have a particular opportunity to "provide a singular atmosphere where women examine and evaluate their lives as women" because everything from curriculum to student leadership can be directed to the needs of women. For women of color, as Bell Scott reminds us, education can empower women only if they first have access to it and if it rids itself of both sexism and racism; educational institutions must become truly pluralistic.

By 1983, when, as Patricia Graham points out in her keynote address, the women's movement reached the age of the traditional college student—eighteen to twenty—a conference on women's issues and/or women's education was part of a major educational movement. Beginning in the 1970s, several conferences addressed specific, primarily curricular issues. The 1972 Wingspread conference, "Women's Higher Education: Some Unanswered Questions," dealt with sexist barriers to women in education and the need for further research in women's development as a factor in their educational experience. Women's studies courses and programs, then in fledgling stages at many colleges and universities, were seen as increasingly effective counters to effects of sexism in educational programs. In 1973, a Mills College conference titled "Beyond Sexism: Educating Women for the Future" challenged educators to consider women's issues as human issues, and began to encourage the inclusion of information on women in the standard liberal arts curriculum. This movement, later called "mainstreaming," was the specific focus of a 1981 Wingspread conference, "Liberal Learning and the New Scholarship on Women." The growth of such scholarship in a variety of academic disciplines since the 1970s makes alterations of the traditional curriculum unavoidable. The Wingspread participants made specific recommendations to various sectors of the educational community.

An exploration of the assumptions and challenges of the Stephens symposium in 1983 should not suggest that all issues in women's education are agreed upon and resolved in this book. The symposium raised more questions than it answered, and it issues no resolutions or specific recommendations. However, several directions for education are clearly articulated here. One is a simple acceptance of change—in curriculum, in attitudes toward women students, in environment. Another is a deeper recognition of the impact of social values and assumptions on educational policy and content, and the understanding that these are arbitrary rather than immutable. Perhaps most immediately necessary is collaboration among those who are concerned about women's education: the sharing and support that have characterized the methods of the women's movement. None of us who planned the symposium expected the deep excitement that resulted from this particular collaboration. In the final moments of the final symposium session, a Stephens student summarized the impact on her of the speeches and discussions by saying she realized there was a place for her as a scholar and a feminist. She, and we all, understood that all of us are present at a quiet, important revolution that we all must, collectively, bring to fruition.

Patricia Albjerg Graham

The Cult of True Womanhood: Past and Present

The feminist movement has come of age—eighteen years of age by some calculations or twenty by others.* The feminist movement faces all the perplexities that many eighteen- or twenty-year-olds encounter when they begin to participate fully in this society. I would like to discuss these perplexities. I believe that the feminist movement has had a great impact upon all of us, both women and men. I also believe that for both women and men the impact of the feminist movement has been largely beneficial.

However, at this time I'll discuss three changes in expectations for women that have occurred in this society over the last century. I want to begin by talking about expectations for women in the mid-nineteenth century, views that shaped the lives of the founders of Stephens one hundred and fifty years ago. Then I want to shift to discuss expectations for women in America in the mid-years of the twentieth century, 1940–1960. Finally, I want to talk about the expectations that we hold for young women of the 1980s.

Our views of what women, particularly those women who were middle class, should do and what they should be, what attributes they should exhibit, have changed a good deal. The experience for women over the last century has been toward increased options both for their attitudes and for their behavior. Given the choice of restricted vs. expanded

―――――――
*I am indebted to a number of persons for assistance in the preparation of these remarks, especially Victor W. Henningsen III. In addition, a number of colleagues at the Harvard Graduate School of Education listened patiently and advised wisely during discussions of these issues.

Patricia Albjerg Graham at a press conference after her keynote address.

alternatives for women, I unhesitatingly choose broader alternatives. Nonetheless, these greater choices have had their difficulties as well, and this plethora of alternatives has brought deep discomfort to many modern women, just as the bounded restrictions brought frustration to their mothers and grandmothers.

The higher educational institutions in this country have played a unique role in forming women's conceptions of themselves and in mediating society's expectations for women. Let us, then, review the role colleges played for women. To what extent did college attendance serve to modify, exempt, or reinforce societal views regarding expectations for women?

I raise these issues both as historical questions regarding higher education and as a contemporary matter. Are our colleges and universities today reinforcing or altering society's expectations for women? Or do colleges today have any influence at all on women students? Are they relevant to women's lives? What should they be doing? In order to approach some kind of answer to our question, we need to establish what society has expected women, principally middle-class women, to do and to be.

Let us begin by considering these matters in the nineteenth century: The American historian, Barbara Welter, wrote in 1966 an article that has triggered much comment and speculation, "The Cult of True Womanhood." I am sure that it is familiar to many of you. In it she argued that the prescriptive literature of the mid-nineteenth century told women, mostly middle-class women, that they should embody four critical qualities. These were piety, purity, submissiveness, and domesticity. Clearly not all women manifested this quartet of virtues, but Welter argued that the conventional wisdom of the nineteenth century was that those four characteristics were desirable for a woman either to attain or at a minimum, to seek.[1]

At the same time that women were supposed to be aspiring to be pious, pure, submissive, and domestic, they were also having their first opportunity to attend college. Oberlin admitted women in 1837, being the first college in the United States to permit coeducation. By the middle of the century a

1. Barbara Welter, "The Cult of True Womanhood, 1820–1860."

number of institutions were offering work of a collegiate grade both to women alone and, increasingly, in settings with men students too. A prime spur to the opening of college doors to women was the Civil War, beginning in 1861 and continuing for four decimating years. The war itself, drawing the collegiate men away from their campuses to the battlefields, and the economic consequences of the war, Reconstruction in the South, and profound financial uncertainty in the North combined to diminish the number of young men seeking to spend four years in college. With such a shortage of male students, a number of colleges were willing to enroll the only other source of tuition-paying students, women.

Thus the early college women understood that they were challenging the canons of true womanhood by deciding to attend college. They knew that their piety might be affected, that their purity was endangered by attendance away from their familial environs, that their submissiveness might be undermined by the necessity to study new material that might challenge existing dogmas or views, and finally, that their future domesticity might be threatened by becoming so learned and even worse, so nontraditional, that they might not either seek or be sought for matrimony. In fact, the early generations of college women married at much lower rates than the population at large. One study has found that only half the graduates of the women's colleges in the late nineteenth century married, roughly the same proportion of women Ph.D.s in the mid-twentieth century.[2]

Probably what is most significant about the experience of the nineteenth-century woman college student, in distinction to that of the twentieth-century one, was that attendance at college seemed to exempt many of them from the expectations of the cult of true womanhood. This occurred primarily for two reasons: one, because such small numbers of either men or women were enrolled that college itself was a deviant choice and two, because attending college flew in the face of several of the behaviors that women were supposed to exhibit.

As Marion Talbot, class of 1880 at Boston University, recalled many years later, "Three questions had to be faced by any thoughtful young woman who in 1880 had a college or

2. Roberta Frankfort, *Collegiate Women: Domesticity and Career in Turn of the Century America*, pp. 54–59, 112–13.

university degree: First, what especial value had a college degree been to her individually and personally? Second, if there were value in such a degree, how best could she assist in forwarding the aims and ambitions of other young women who also wished such training? Third, how best could she fit herself into her community and play the part in its life and program which was at once her interest and her evident obligation?"[3] All this was very different from the injunction to be pious, pure, submissive, and domestic.

Women college students made up a tiny fraction of the age group in 1870, but what is also very important, men college students also made up a very small fraction of the age group then. In 1860 about one percent of the age group was in college, and the proportion of these who were women was very small indeed. A decade later, the one that included the Civil War, the proportion of the eighteen- to twenty-one-year-olds who were in college was half again as much, 1.68 percent. What is most striking about that increase, however, is that already 21 percent of the undergraduates were women. A decade later, 1880, almost three percent of the age group were in college, and 32 percent of them were women. Undergraduates of whom 32 percent were female is the same proportion that was true for the U.S. in the early 1950s. The great difference was that in 1880, roughly one hundred years ago, slightly less than three percent of the age group was in college. In the 1950s nearly 30 percent of the age group was in college. Thus, the late nineteenth century students who attended college were a tiny fraction of the population, and by virtue of being such a small group they became exempt from many of the strictures of the society. They enjoyed some of the benefits of an elite, of a group who somehow did not have to play by the same rules as the rest of America.[4]

College attendance for men in the nineteenth century had a different consequence than college attendance did for women. Fundamentally, it did not contradict society's expectations for manliness. It might not support them, but it did not contradict them. Middle-class men in the nineteenth cen-

3. Marion Talbot and Lois Kimball Rosenberry, *The History of the American Association of University Women, 1881–1931*, p. 7.
4. A table of these statistics may be found in Patricia Albjerg Graham, "Expansion and Exclusion: A History of Women in American Higher Education," p. 766.

tury were supposed to prepare themselves in some way to support themselves and their families successfully as adults. Clearly college attendance was not required to do this, but few believed that college would be a decided hindrance. Therefore, the decision to attend college for men did not challenge the existing conceptions for men as the same decision did for women. Men were not supposed to be pious, pure, submissive, and domestic, so an activity that made the acquisition of those qualities less likely was not threatening to them.

One important consequence for women, particularly for the small number of professional women, in the late nineteenth and early twentieth centuries was the development of a series of separate feminine networks. Patricia Palmieri has written a fascinating study of the faculty at Wellesley College arrestingly titled, "In Adamless Eden."[5] Their feminist and feminine culture in the years 1890 to 1910 give evidence of the way that these early college women who became professors rejected at least two of the fundamental canons of the cult of true womanhood of their youth, namely they did not achieve conventional domesticity since none married, although all participated in households that held great significance for them. Neither were they submissive in the usual sense since they engaged in vigorous discussions with each other on various academic and intellectual matters. One might argue that, in fact, they pursued their own form of domesticity in their carefully structured and supportive community. Similarly one might believe that they engaged in a version of submissive behavior in their unwillingness to participate (for those few for whom the option ever arose) in the entirely male world of the research universities, such as Harvard, Yale, or Columbia. Few have challenged the purity of these ladies. By the end of the nineteenth century in the environments in which these women lived "piety" was out of fashion as a religious expression so they were exempt from that too. For some of them the energies that previously had been committed to religious issues had been transformed into social reformist zeal.

The old expectations continued to have meaning for some of the college women, of course. The exemption was nei-

5. Patricia Ann Palmieri, "In Adamless Eden: A Social Portrait of the Academic Community at Wellesley College, 1875–1920."

ther uniform nor complete. As Joyce Antler has observed in her article, "After College, What?: New Graduates and the Family Claim," the college women of the late nineteenth century whom she studied all recognized that there were many more options in life than those embodied in the traditional virtues of piety, purity, submissiveness, and domesticity.[6] What many of these women found was that college opened many new possibilities and ideas for them, but society, including the society of their families, made it difficult for many of them to organize their own lives in ways to take advantage of these entrancing options. Many reported illness, depression, and despondency on their return to their home communities from college. In their post-college lives convention reigned and, for many, the interlude between college and determining their subsequent professional course was painful. Two of the best-known examples of women who found that transition extremely difficult but who subsequently triumphed professionally were Jane Addams, who eventually established Hull House in Chicago, and M. Carey Thomas, who became president of Bryn Mawr. Similarly several Wellesley alumnae of the class of 1897 who wrote back to the college about their lives as wives and mothers, apparently felt compelled both to justify their choices while admitting that their lives were not as full as they had hoped. One wrote, "The rest of my report is distressingly negative. . . . Public services? Nothing greater than an underling in hospital fairs" or another, "I have done nothing wonderful . . . two children."[7] But perhaps their partial exemption from the traditional canons of true womanhood were best expressed by a Vassar graduate who wrote, "We college girls are made to feel that we are different."[8]

Indeed, they were different. By the mid years of the next century, 1940–1960, how different were college women? What was the set of expectations by which women of that generation were to live their lives? To what extent did college attendance influence either those expectations or women's adherence to them?

6. Joyce Antler, "'After College, What?': New Graduates and the Family Claim," pp. 409–33.
7. Ibid., p. 429.
8. "Editorial," *The Vassar Miscellany* 34 (1902) 33, quoted in Antler, "'After College, What?'" p. 411.

By the mid-twentieth century, college women were no longer different. In 1940 nearly 15 percent of the eighteen- to twenty-one-year-olds were undergraduates, and of those students, 40 percent were women.[9] Although the proportion of young people attending college had increased significantly from the 8 percent in 1920, the proportion of women among the undergraduates had declined from a high of 47 percent in 1920 to the 40 percent in 1940.[10] At the beginning of World War II, then, we were beginning to see a new trend that developed during the ensuing twenty years: college attendance was becoming increasingly common, especially for young men. Clearly, participating in World War II from 1941 to 1945 affected college enrollment for men, but similarly that participation made available college attendance in the late 1940s through the GI Bill for ex-servicemen, almost entirely men, some of whom would not otherwise have attended college. There were 1.5 million college students in 1940, 2.3 million in 1950, and 3.6 million in 1960.[11] The numbers of college students so substantially increased in the period that no middle-class woman could consider herself different by virtue of her college attendance in the mid-twentieth century. By the latter years of the century a middle-class woman was becoming different if she had not gone to college.

"Difference" was increasingly becoming a suspect characteristic for Americans who sought full participation in American life. The cult of conformity that overcame America in the first two thirds of the twentieth century probably had its roots in the Americanization campaigns of the early years of the century when immigrants were coming to the United States in large numbers and when the widely held view was that they should be assimilated into American society. For many immigrants *assimilation* was something that they equated with participation in the favorable economic opportunities that seemed better in the United States than in the nation from which they had come. The manifestation of

9. Graham, "Expansion and Exclusion," p. 766.
10. Ibid.
11. U.S. Bureau of the Census, Current Population Reports, *Population Characteristics*, Series P-20, #374 (Washington, D.C.: U.S. Government Printing Office, 1782); *Historical Statistics of the United States* (Washington, D.C.: U.S. Government Printing Office, 1976), p. 383.

assimilation, however, was frequently a disdain and sometimes a discarding of the cultural traditions of their heritage in favor of what they took to be the new American standards. Most of these new Americans wanted to be middle class. Often they believed their sons would be middle class and American before they felt obligated to assure that their daughters would be as well. One way to become American and middle class was to follow the standards of American behavior that were becoming increasingly comprehensive in their applications to many Americans.

Despite the trauma of the economic recession of the 1930s, a common cultural standard was emerging by 1940. Class differences were being minimized as both the lower and upper classes gravitated toward the attitudes and beliefs associated with the middle class. Regionalism played a diminishing role in American life. Accents, except for Southern and a few Brooklyn or New England ones, began to disappear from American speech. Even ethnic differences were reduced as Jews anglicized their names and Slavs and Scandinavians dropped syllables and unwieldy consonants from theirs.

The peak of cultural homogenization probably came about during World War II when the common experience of military service, much more widespread for American men than World War I had been and certainly much more unifying than the Civil War had been, brought together Irish-Americans from Boston with Hoosier Protestants. Even some of the traditional distinctions between officers and enlisted men and their distinct social-class origins blurred during World War II under the pressure of mass mobilization. Betty Grable and Rita Hayworth were popular pinups with a very large portion of the male population. *Life* was a magazine with appeal for many GI's as well as for lawyers and for shopkeepers. By 1950 listening to network radio was a national experience for Americans. Comparable adventures on television were approaching with even fewer opportunities for a variety of channels on the TV screen than radio had provided for different stations. Local newspapers were failing, and many cities soon found themselves with only one paper where a decade or two earlier they had had several from which to choose. Big purveyors of information were getting larger; the small ones were dropping by the wayside. The homogenization of American culture had become so noticeable that by the early 1950s Will Herberg and others were arguing for cultural pluralism as an antidote to the monotony of American life.[12]

In this milieu there were, of course, a revised set of expectations for middle-class women, and they were much more uniformly applied than previous ones since many more Americans then either considered themselves or aspired to be middle class. One way to achieve that pinnacle was to have your daughter follow the mid-twentieth century canons of true womanhood. The constellation of virtues to which these women were expected to aspire were youth, appearance, acquiescence, and domesticity. Every woman was supposed to enhance her youth and her appearance and to foster her natural predilection for acquiescence and domesticity. The parallel between these qualities and those previously noted as the female virtues a century earlier (piety, purity, submissiveness, and domesticity) is considerable and pointed in many minds to the legitimacy of the persistence of these qualities as natural or divinely right. Yet piety was not important for the secular, twentieth-century woman. Neither was purity, particularly after the availability of effective contraception. For many Americans the fabled emancipation of women in the twentieth century amounted to a rejection of those two nineteenth-century virtues and adoption of the twentieth-century one: acquiescence. One should not submit, but one should acquiesce. There was a subtle difference between the two, placing a premium upon a woman's tact. Finally, the eternal theme of domesticity recurred. The American woman of the mid-twentieth century was to appear young, beautiful, and ardent on demand. She was also to find happiness in her home. Many found that combination difficult.

Unlike the nineteenth century's prescriptive behavior for women, the mid-twentieth century's was not in conflict with college attendance. In fact, undergraduate study was either consistent with or irrelevant to it. To be an undergraduate became proper youthful behavior for a young woman, whose appearance was not harmed by such a step. The posture of any student should be acquiescent, not assertive. In addition, college was frequently considered the ideal place to

12. Will Herberg, *Protestant, Catholic, Jew.*

meet the one with whom the domestic life would be shared. At the end of this era of the mid-twentieth century a woman reporter on the *New York Times* described the college girl of that period: "After four years of studying everything from ancient art to modern psychology, the average college girl views her future through a wedding band. Despite compelling evidence [already the evidence was accumulating that the expectations for young women did not meet the reality of a woman's life] that she will be working at 35, by choice or necessity, today's 21-year-old woman has difficulty looking beyond the ceremonies of her own marriage and her babies' christenings."[13] College had begun to play the role that high school had in the lives of women at the turn of the century, for many simply a pleasant interlude on the way to growing up. It was an educational experience that prosperous and middle-class families sought for their daughters, an experience that all considered fully consistent with society's highest expectations for women.

Graduate school, however, was a different matter. For most women, the psychological and financial factors considered in that decision were much more serious than those for college. Fundamentally this was true because graduate school was seen not as valuable general education, which was useful to the enlightened citizen, but rather it was seen (although rarely stated as such) as intensely vocational. One went to graduate school because if one did and completed the curriculum successfully, then one would be able to get certain distinctive and generally prestigious jobs. Certainly not all jobs of that sort required graduate school—without any graduate work, one could become president of General Motors when that was a booming company—but one could not be a lawyer, physician, professor, or even an advanced teacher without graduate study. In the post-World-War-II years the number of men going to graduate school increased dramatically, particularly as young men of middle-class and lower-middle-class backgrounds found entry into the professions. Women, who had received 15 percent of the doctorates awarded in 1920 and 18 percent of them in 1930 had dropped to only 10 percent in 1950 and in 1960. The relative

---

13. Marilyn Bender, "College Girl Often Sees No Future But Marriage," *New York Times*, 26 March 1962.

decline of women was indicative of the substantially larger number of men who were seeking these degrees. The proportions of women in the prestigious professional schools, especially law and medicine, were even lower.[14]

Graduate school by the mid-twentieth century provided the key to the professions, and one element of the great drive to become middle class was the desire also to become a professional. This current widely recognized in American popular culture, even permeated the elite scholarly literature, as the 1963 issue of *Daedalus* on the professions indicated. Kenneth Lynn introduced that issue with the statement, "Everywhere in American life, professions are triumphant."[15] David Halberstam published his paean to the leaders of the sixties, *The Best and the Brightest*, and praised that unity of intelligence, rationality, and tough decisions that supposedly embodied professionalism.[16] Needless to say, all the best and the brightest were men.

The mid-twentieth-century female virtues were seriously at odds with professionalism. It is difficult to imagine anything more hostile to professionalism than eroticism. Professionalism supposedly implies a commitment to rationality and rigorous objective standards. Eroticism, with its component of sensuality, is the antithesis of such rationality. Yet if a woman were to be truly a woman in mid-twentieth-century America, she had to have some qualities considered erotic. The possession of those characteristics so necessary to her definition as a woman denied her professionalism. While it was not a bad thing for a man to be sexy or good-looking, those qualities were not as essential to his self-definition. In those years discussions of problems of sexual dysfunctionalism typically focused on women's difficulties: they were frigid; they failed either to achieve orgasm or the right kind of orgasm. Lundberg and Farnham discussed these and other "problems of the modern woman" in *Modern Woman, The Lost Sex*, a volume that found a wide readership among educated women in the years after it was published in 1947.[17] Only

14. Graham, "Expansion and Exclusion," p. 766.
15. Kenneth S. Lynn, "Introduction," *Daedalus* 92 (1963): 649–54.
16. David Halberstam, *The Best and the Brightest* (New York: Random House, 1972).
17. Ferdinand Lundberg and Marynia Foot Farnham, *Modern Woman, The Lost Sex*.

later did sexual problems for men achieve prominence in the popular literature, and then they were frequently blamed on women's new, inappropriately aggressive behavior.

A successful man, in the mid-twentieth century, was to be assertive, and it was widely understood that he would—and probably even should—place a higher priority upon the demands of his job than his responsibilities within his family. For him to fail to do so would lead many to question his professional commitment, a surrogate for his manliness. Yet just the reverse were the expectations for women. In that era an assertive woman was likely to be called a bitch, or worse, and one who placed her job above the needs of her family was violating a fundamental standard of society. Domesticity reigned triumphant as a goal, though not as a reality, in women's lives, and they continued to seek to appear youthful, attractive, and acquiescent.

The sixties were a decade of tumult for the nation. They began on a hopeful note with the election of a new president with a charming and entrancing family, particularly his wife, who had had a career—not a very imposing one, but a career, nonetheless—before she married him and began to bear his children. She represented many new, emerging virtues for American women. Jackie Kennedy was beautiful, intelligent, sophisticated, devoted to her children, and until the tragedy struck in Dallas in November 1963, many believed that she represented the new, classy life-style that hopeful Americans thought might be theirs. Their dream was short; Camelot remained a mythic entity.

Kennedy's presidency, brief though it was, inaugurated a coming of age of the young, persons who reached maturity in a world shaped not by the Great Depression of the 1930s but by the affluence of postwar America. As Kennedy had urged them, many undertook to do something for their country, not just something for themselves. Not all of their elders were pleased with the projects they undertook.

First came major activity in the civil rights arena. The Civil Rights Act of 1964 followed the harsh actions of white police against blacks in the South. The following year Martin Luther King led thousands in a march from Selma to Montgomery that attracted many liberals, both blacks and whites, from outside Alabama. One of them, a working-class white woman from Detroit, Viola Liuzzo, was killed, ambushed in her car by white Southerners who believed she should have stayed home.

Staying home proved to be one of the most divisive issues of the decade. Hard on the heels of the civil rights movement, which had been initiated by blacks seeking full participation for themselves in the society, came efforts by women, mostly white, middle-class women, who began first by challenging the primacy of domesticity as a virtue to which they should aspire. Viola Liuzzo had probably not read the book published two years earlier, *The Feminine Mystique*, but her actions in the civil rights movement represented the change that was coming upon women who made this critique a best-seller.[18] Its author, Betty Friedan, a housewife in Rockland County, New York, argued that the media were trying to create an environment in which women were placed on a pedestal and in that isolated, awkward but supposedly admirable position, their opportunities for full participation in the society were impaired.

Both men and women worked together in the civil rights movement, both black and white men and women initially. Later in the decade both men and women worked together on college campuses in the student protests, but women increasingly came to the conviction that in these efforts, they should, as the slogan went, "make policy, not coffee." Generally that was a conviction that the men did not share. Following the deaths in the spring of 1968 of Martin Luther King and of Robert F. Kennedy, the fragile coalitions split. Blacks and whites no longer worked collaboratively on civil rights issues. As the student protest movements on the campuses turned increasingly toward anti-Viet Nam activities, the women lost what leadership they had had. Women, mostly white, mostly middle class, and mostly beyond college age, became involved with the women's movement. *Feminist*, initially a derisive term, gradually became a descriptive one.

At first the women's movement had looked as if it might attract only a following from the radical fringe. It was identified with bra burning, attacks on conventional feminine activities (Kinder, Kuche, Kirche), and widespread allegations of discrimination against women in all areas of American so-

---

18. Betty Friedan, *The Feminine Mystique*.

ciety. The initial charges were so fundamental and so broad that many women, unsure what the consequences would be of aligning themselves with such a movement, cautiously waited.

By the end of the turbulent 1960s, however, the women's movement was achieving a new legitimacy. In 1969 both Yale and Princeton, bastions of collegiate conservatism, had admitted their first classes of women students. Both institutions argued that it was morally wrong to deprive young women, who they now argued were academically and otherwise equal with men, of an education at Yale and Princeton. Actually in both cases an important component of the decision to become coeducational was the recognition that some of the most talented young men who had been admitted to either Yale or Princeton had decided to go to institutions that were coeducational. The action of Yale and Princeton, however, gave a face validity to the notion that these prestigious and traditional institutions were willing to accept women into their student bodies. Naturally they would not do so initially on an equal basis with men (there were quotas limiting the number of women who could be admitted to a proportion substantially under 50 percent of the undergraduates), but admit them they did.

By 1970 *Time* magazine, that quintessential journal of the middle class, provided evidence that the women's movement was now news for everyone, not just an aberration limited to a few freaks in New York, San Francisco, and other exotic spots outside the heartland of America. For its August 31, 1970, cover (the back-to-school issue, perhaps) it pictured Kate Millett, author of the new book, *Sexual Politics*.[19] Although the book, begun initially as a Ph.D. thesis in the Columbia University English Department, was much too abstruse for most readers, the title caught on, symbolizing for many the manipulation of women by men into acceptance of values that women would neither have chosen for themselves nor believed were beneficial for them.

During much of the sixties and the seventies, I believe that it would be impossible to identify the qualities that many women or men would have agreed characterized "true womanhood." Gradually I think we are moving from that

19. *Time*, 31 August 1970. Kate Millett, *Sexual Politics*.

period of uncertainty. This evening I want to propose four qualities that encompass what many in this society, both women and men, believe that women should be. The woman of the 1980s should be attractive, active, ambitious, and ambivalent.

The qualities of the eighties differed significantly from those of the mid-years of the century, an evidence of the power of the women's movement itself. The first quality of the mid-century, youth, became for the late twentieth century, attractive. Certainly one of the messages of the last two decades was that while it was certainly desirable for a woman to be young, even more important was for a woman to be attractive. The woman of thirty or forty, or even God forbid, fifty, had an obligation to preserve and enhance her attractiveness. Oil of Olay was specifically designed for those of us who are older to keep our skin attractive, as the advertisements with women with slight, lilting foreign accents attest. In an earlier era one accepted the natural beauty that came with youth; in the present one a woman has a perennial obligation to make herself attractive, regardless of age. In my mother's or my grandmother's generation, at forty-eight I could have expected to wear shapeless cotton housedresses, become dowdy and no longer feel obligated to try and fit into a size 10 dress. Today, despite the efforts of some authors to argue otherwise, such as Susie Orbach, *Fat is a Feminist Issue,* the reigning best-seller is by another woman, like Orbach also a feminist, Jane Fonda, whose workout book has been in the *New York Times* best-seller list for fifty-six weeks.[20] All of us have an obligation to work at being attractive and being fit.

Secondly, in addition to being attractive, we must also be active. Being active is, of course, related to being attractive, but it goes beyond simply physical activity, much as that is praised. Aerobic exercise, jogging, swimming are all activities for the woman of the eighties. For some of us who recently got into a leotard for the first time since college physical education some years ago, there was a sense of terrible déjà vu, as if this were an experience that was appropriate

---

20. Susie Orbach, *Fat is a Feminist Issue: The Anti-Diet Guide to Permanent Weight Loss* (New York: Berkeley Press, 1979); and, Jane Fonda, *Jane Fonda's Workout Book* (New York: Simon and Schuster, 1981).

for youngsters but why must the rest of us still have this inflicted upon us! Partly we are active to make us attractive, the first goal of the woman of the eighties, and partly we are active to preserve the flexibility of our youth and enhance our appearance, goals of the mid-twentieth century woman. But we are active for another very important reason as well. The contemplative or sedentary model is no longer one that is highly regarded. The woman whose energies are given to writing letters—even to the sick; to reading—even broadly and in esoteric literatures; to needlework—even if it is lovely; to painting water colors—even if they are breathtaking; such a woman, who in the Victorian era would have been highly praised for embracing the qualities of true womanhood, would be disparaged today as not being active enough. She need not wear British Brevitts and hike briskly through the woods, but she does need to move, to participate.

If the first two characteristics defined the way she should look, be attractive, and the mode in which she should act, be active, the third and fourth determine the attitudes she should hold. The third replaces the submissiveness of the nineteenth century and the acquiescence of the mid-twentieth with ambition. No longer is a woman to arrange her world around a man's. Now she is to have goals for her life, and she is expected to admit them frankly and more than simply admit them, she is supposed to act to attain them. Many women expect to achieve their ambition through employment, although for some women ambition is not simply in terms of vocation. One recent study of Barnard College undergraduates found that only 6 percent expect never to work while 53 percent expect to work full time. The balance expected to work full time and part time, arranging their working schedule around the needs of their families.[21] A Roper poll recently reported that twice as many women are working full time now as ten years ago, now 35 percent vs. 18 percent at the beginning of the 1970s.[22] In October 1982, the Department of Labor revealed that the total number

21. Mira Komarovsky, "College Women and Careers," *New York Times*, 23 January 1981.
22. Judy Klemsrud, "Survey Finds Major Shifts in Attitudes of Women," *New York Times*, 13 March 1980.

of women working has risen 95 percent in the last twenty years.[23] Given the high unemployment rates, especially for women, these current figures are probably lower than what women would like.

Perhaps even more indicative of the ambition that young women, especially, now feel comfortable in expressing is the sentiment of a senior at the Emma Willard school, who explained to a researcher who inquired about her plans, "I am going to be VERY SUCCESSFUL and at 25 I am going to retire and have a family." Such is the level of realism among some of the young! Only slightly more realistic are these two examples of changing ambitions among Radcliffe alumnae, the first from the class of 1969, "While I was at Radcliffe, I thought about choosing a safe profession, one that I could leave in order to have children and then resume again later." The second is from the class of 1979, "I want a career that will allow me to be financially independent. I'd like to get married, but it is important for me to have a professional identity first." The most popular academic majors for Radcliffe students in the first group were English, history, and philosophy but for the second, those who want a career and financial independence, the most popular majors were biology, economics, and government.[24]

Young women, especially, anticipate a life that will bring an interesting and compelling job. With such, they believe, will come fulfillment. Most undergraduate women today have never faced the overt discrimination in employment encountered by their elders. Many women in graduate and professional schools have not faced it either. Perhaps they never will, but the persistence of the female wage at 59 percent of the male wage is discouraging in this respect. For most young women immediately out of college or professional school, the job opportunities are remarkably similar to those for young men of the same academic preparation. Perhaps what is most important, young women's and young men's expectations for career possibilities in first jobs are also remarkably similar, and in that similarity we find a profound difference with the past.

23. "More Women Work at Traditional Male Jobs," *New York Times*, 15 November 1982.
24. Patricia Albjerg Graham, "Women and Higher Education: From Whence Have We Come?" Address delivered at Stanford University, 6 May 1981.

The attractive, active, ambitious woman of the 1980s has one other characteristic, one that society expects her to have and one that is, in fact, widely shared among women of all ages today. She is ambivalent. Her ambivalence in the eighties replaces the domesticity of her mother and her female ancestors. She is ambivalent, of course, because neither she nor anyone else knows how to combine successfully her ambition with her desire for a compelling personal life. If her personal life is to include a family, either a husband, or husband and children, or just children, adjustments must be made in her expectations for her career. Just what adjustments are those? What agencies in the society have responsibility for assuring those adjustments? Is she expected to make these adjustments all alone without any help from the outside, from social institutions, from her employer, or, most of all, from the father of her children? If there is one thing that women learned from the women's movement of the last two decades, it is that the problems that they thought were theirs individually were actually part of a larger set of social problems that affected them all. Yet this question of the appropriate balance between career or employment and family life is one to which women are still seeking individual, not collective, solutions.

The ambivalence of women, characteristic of nearly all generations today, is perhaps most clearly seen among those who came to maturity during the uncertainty of the last two decades and who found themselves as young women just out of college supported by the society to seek an important job or significant post-graduate study. Many of them did so successfully and now in their mid or late thirties or even early forties, having forthrightly pursued an elusive goal called "success" with its concomitants of money, prestige, and recognition, they discover that other elements of their lives need attention. For those who are married, there is the question of children. Their biological clock is running down. But what will children do to their life-style? The one answer to that question is that children will change their life-style, but in what ways? For those who are not married, there may also be the question of children, either of their own, or adopted or jointly reared with the child's natural parent. In any case, well-educated women are concerned about the matter. The higher the level of a woman's education, the fewer children she is likely to have and the later in life she is likely to have them.

At least as important as the question of children in fostering the ambivalence that a woman feels, is her uncertainty regarding the adult or adults whom she will love. How important should that relationship be? To what extent should one make accommodations to the needs of another? Traditionally issues of morality have been expressed in terms of one's rights (I have the right to do *x* or *y* or *z*) but recent work by Carol Gilligan has revealed that women often view these matters in terms of responsibilities.[25] For the women, then, the question is likely to be, "What is my responsibility to myself and to the one whom I love?" Most do not find the answer immediately apparent.

An ongoing study of undergraduate women in the so-called "Seven Sister" colleges (Barnard, Bryn Mawr, Mt. Holyoke, Radcliffe, Smith, Vassar, and Wellesley) finds that most expect to have a very good career in a prestigious profession and have two or three children. The women undergraduates' goals are very similar to those of a sample of men undergraduates at Harvard. In addition, less than 3 percent of the women surveyed are interested in traditional women's careers, such as teaching or social work. On the basis of very tentative findings the seniors seem to believe that they can work full time and have their children while the freshmen are more inclined to believe that some modifications in working (either taking time out from employment or working part time—both sure to reduce opportunites for career ambitions to be realized) are required.[26]

What is obvious is that in the older generation of women, ones now in their forties and fifties, the opportunities for combining successful career and parenthood were limited. Whether those limitations occurred because women and society in general discouraged such combinations or because women were not prepared to undertake such responsibilities is unclear. Undoubtedly both factors contribute to an explanation. Now it is reasonably clear that women are prepared to undertake such responsibilities and are educated through undergraduate and professional schools to do so.

---

25. Carol Gilligan, *In a Different Voice: Psychological Theory and Women's Development*.
26. Diane Casselberry Manuel, "Study Shows College Women Hope to Combine Career and Family," *Christian Science Monitor*, 29 December 1982.

Whether society is ready for these women when they are middle aged to have the same opportunities as middle-aged men is much less clear.

One may observe that while ambivalence may be characteristic of many modern women, it is not socially sanctioned. Women may be ambivalent, but society does not expect them to be ambivalent the way they are expected to be active, attractive, and ambitious. I would argue that indeed society at the present time does expect women to be ambivalent about the commitments to job and to personal life. This ambivalence is expected, I believe, because we are in a transitional period in which we as a society have not yet resolved what, ultimately, we believe should be the priorities of adult lives for persons of both sexes. In the face of this ambiguity, we prescribe ambivalence for women.

Again the question returns: to what extent does higher education have any role to play in affecting these expectations for women? The first observation is that women now constitute a majority of the undergraduates, both among the conventional age group (age eighteen to twenty-one) and among the total. There are also lots more undergraduates now than there were twenty years ago. In 1960 there were 3.6 million students enrolled in college; in 1970, a phenomenal rise to 8 million, and in 1980, 10 million. Secondly, college or university attendance today is a necessary prerequisite for most prestigious (and some not so prestigious) careers. Enrollments of women in professional schools, such as law, medicine, and business, have jumped from under 5 percent in 1960 to over 30 percent today. Still substantial but less dramatic increases have occurred for women Ph.D.s, from 10 percent in 1960 to over 25 percent now.[27]

Higher education has continued to play an important role in preparing women so that they can meet entry-level requirements for jobs, but it has not been as helpful to them in providing adult examples in their own institutions of women who have successfully combined career and family. The proportion of women in senior, as opposed to junior,

27. U.S. Census Bureau, Current Population Reports, *Population Characteristics*, Series P-20, #374 (September 1982). See also, Patricia Albjerg Graham, "Expansion and Exclusion" 766, and U.S. Bureau of the Census, *Historical Statistics of the United States* (Washington, D.C.: U.S. Government Printing Office, 1976), pp. 385–86.

positions in faculties and administrations has not grown dramatically, although it has increased. Men faculty continue to be substantially more likely to be tenured than women (70 percent versus 49 percent), and men faculty continue to be paid more than women in the same ranks (about $5,000 for full professors in private universities). Higher education today gets a woman started, but it does not give her much guidance about what to do after she has begun.[28]

One of the most interesting aspects of these new expectations for women in the late twentieth century is the degree of convergence with expectations for men in the same period. Some might call this evidence of creeping androgyny. Certainly men of the nineteenth century were not supposed to be pious, pure, submissive, and domestic. Neither were men of the mid-twentieth century expected to share the virtues of youth, appearance, acquiescence, and domesticity. Now, however, the gap is much less. Men today want to be attractive; Grecian Formula 16 is a big seller on the male market. They are also supposed to be active, not just in youthful football as was the case twenty years ago, but through fitness programs involving even the middle aged. When Dr. Paul Dudley White began exercising in Boston in the 1950s, he was nearly alone. Now the paths along the Charles River are clogged with trim, gray-haired and balding men, as well as young ones, who are jogging to stay fit, keep their weight down, and lower their blood pressure. Not surprisingly, men still are ambitious, though the attention given to type A personalities has had the effect of modifying their stated goals slightly. The workaholic is not the universal stamp of approval that it once was. Finally, even men are becoming ambivalent. What ought the balance be in their lives between their jobs and their personal lives? In previous generations very little conscious thought was given to that equation, but today many men, either those who have the issue triggered by the newly popular midlife crisis or those who became involved with one of the feminist, ambitious professional women or simply those who for whatever reasons are now able to express their intention for a close family life—all face

---

28. Tom Jackman, "Female Professors Gain Little Ground," *New York Times*, 9 January 1983. See also, "Men and Women 1982–83 Salaries Compared," Chronicle Survey, in *The Chronicle of Higher Education*, 26 January 1983.

the question of responsibility for personal lives and for family demands too. The company no longer can make unilateral assignments for men to move from Toledo to Texarkana. Promotions of that kind raise men's sense of ambivalence too.

Thus, to conclude, we find the women of today beneficiaries of much broader societally sanctioned options prescribing the ways in which they should spend their adult lives than was true for middle-class American women of earlier generations. We, today, often feel uncertain about these varied opportunities. For our ancestors the issue was one of conforming or breaking the mold into which society had put them. Those alternatives, however difficult, were at least clearer. Relatively few chose to break the mold; most accepted conformity with greater or lesser grace and satisfaction.

Today we face a different issue, different in two ways: for us the range of options—or the course of life—available to us as women is much broader than it was for our female ancestors; for us the determinants of choice are more ambiguous than was the case for our mothers and grandmothers. The opportunities open to us are immensely greater but with such increased alternatives comes the necessity of setting a course. Typically we have expressed these alternative courses in individual terms. We have not recognized that the gains that we have won and that have brought us these alternatives have been achieved through collective action. Many of us now seek to play our futures, confident that our own planning is sufficient. These issues remain imbedded in the fabric of our society, and without support from other women in these decisions—as well as from men—we will be unable to recognize and follow these courses on our own. If we choose to move beyond the conventional through expanded prescriptions, as I suspect that many of us will wish to do, we must rally support for those new paths from many quarters. Acceptance of part-time employment, child-care facilities, flexible time, interrupted career patterns will not come through individual actions but only through collective efforts. We are not in a position to chart a course alone, any more than a single woman was responsible for creating the conditions of the 1960s and 1970s that brought us the women's movement.

Secondly, we must recognize that the inevitable choices

we must make about our course are more ambiguous than those made by the women who chose either career or family a generation ago. Rarely are the decisions presented to us today so clear cut. Commonly they are cloaked in a murky, enigmatic ambiguity. Since the options are not so stark (young women believe that they can have it all, even if they do not know how to arrange it all), then the need for choice is muted. We are under the impression that if we simply "work at it" that "things will eventually work out." No doubt often that is true. Nonetheless, sometimes it is necessary to make distinct choices in the uncertainty that abounds. We are hesitant to make those choices since we are never clear precisely what the consequences or the alternative we choose will be. Furthermore, in making such choices we are assuming responsibility for our own lives. By doing so we no longer can blame whatever difficulties we have upon circumstances that either kept us in the mold or forced us to take dramatic action to break out of it.

Our excuses are gone, and we are assuming full responsibilities for our adult lives. That may be uncomfortable occasionally, but it is decidedly preferable in my view to the alternative. We must rejoice in our options for choice. We must not be paralyzed by them. We must move ahead in our lives, assuming responsibility for our decisions, knowing that unlike previous generations we have more opportunities to decide what we will do, whom we will be. That is a great gift.

Gerda Lerner

The Rise of Feminist Consciousness

Feminist consciousness has been in the past and will increasingly be in the future a prime motor for social change. While women have participated in every movement for social change and often times have been very active and leading in those movements, they have not always done so with feminist consciousness. There is a distinction between woman's participation in movements for social change and woman's participation as *feminists* in movements for social change.

First, however, let us define our terms. I define feminism as feminine consciousness in action: the consciousness of women that they are a segregated group, that they are dominated or subordinated to men in one or more aspects of their lives; that they must unite with other women to define the terms of their own emancipation and to struggle for it; finally, the definition by women of their own goals as a group.

My definition of *feminism* is a system of ideas and practices which assumes that men and women must share equally in the work, in the privileges, in the defining and the dreaming of the world. Feminism assumes that men and women are equal as citizens before the law and as human beings. It does not necessarily assume that they should be striving to wipe out or to minimize biological differences. For some feminists this is implicit in their definition, for others it merely means that biological differences should have no more significance in assigning gender roles than should the color of one's hair or shape of one's nose.

It is useful to notice that feminism has historically consisted of two separate and quite different currents: one, the

Gerda Lerner talks informally with Jo Hartley, editor of *Comment*, and Claire Healey. Hartley and Healey, with Sheila Tobias and Melissa Clapp (student), produced a capsulization of the proceedings called "The Daily Comment" for each of the three days of the symposium.

movement for woman's rights, and two, the movement for women's emancipation.

The woman's rights movement, in its various historical manifestations, is a phase, specific and limited in time and scope, of the broader feminist movement. The woman's rights movement has defined the emancipation of women as the winning of legal and economic rights and privileges. Feminism, on the other hand, embraces all aspects of the emancipation of women, that is any struggle designed to elevate women's status socially, politically, economically, educationally, and in respect to their self concepts. The movement for woman's rights is akin to the civil rights movement of minorities or blacks in this country. It is a movement for equal access to all the opportunities and an equal share in all the institutions of the society as it is. It does not necessarily imply or demand any change in the existing institutions other than that they should be open to women on the basis of equality. But the movement for woman's emancipation always implies a transformation of the institutions and values of the society.

The concept "women's emancipation" embraces three aspects: women's striving for freedom from oppressive restrictions imposed by sex; self-determination, and autonomy. *Freedom from oppressive restrictions imposed by sex* means freedom from natural, biological, as well as from societally imposed restrictions. *Self-determination* means being free to decide one's own destiny, being free to define one's own social role. *Autonomy* means earning one's own status, not being born to it or marrying it. It means financial and social independence, freedom to choose one's life-style. In order for women to have autonomy, the handicap of male orientation, male definition, and male domination of social institutions must first be removed. It is obvious that society must reach a certain level of development before such emancipation can take place and that women's full emancipation has as yet nowhere on earth been accomplished. Women's emancipation cannot be accomplished without incorporating the demands of the woman's rights movement, but the reverse is not the case. Those who teach Women's Studies might find it useful to make these distinctions. They help us to define women's strivings in a much more precise way than does the usual vague use of the term *feminist* for anything and everything that concerns women's struggle for equality with men.

Historically, the rise of feminist consciousness develops in certain distinct stages: 1) the awareness of a wrong; 2) the development of a sense of sisterhood; 3) autonomous definition of goals and strategies for change and 4) the development of an alternate vision of the future.

The awareness of a wrong may seem so obvious a precondition for the rise of consciousness as not to deserve mentioning. But it is in fact quite complex. For example, the starving peasant knows he is starving, but does he know who is to blame or even that he has either the ability or the right to find out who is to blame? Unless certain preconditions are present, it is far more likely that he will accept his condition as he accepts the weather, as natural and God given.

For women confined for millennia within the narrow limits of their family circle, disadvantaged in their access to learning and ignorant of their history, such recognition had to come more slowly. More importantly, women have had to operate within an idea system entirely defined and dominated by male thoughts. Women have been educationally disadvantaged systematically and deliberately since the creation of Western civilization and the invention of writing. All the systems of ideas of Western civilization, the explanations of the world and the cosmos, philosophies, and science have literally been shaped by male thought. Women have been marginal to this process of idea formation, although they have had an input in ways we do not really know. We have not quite traced the form and the manner of the way in which women have influenced thought. The few brave female minds searching to find causes for their condition have somehow had to find the fortitude and insight to challenge male definitions and explanations. There always were these few, the rebels, the challengers of authority and patriarchal wisdom. For hundreds of years the precondition of their coming into being was that they had to be upper class, for only women of that class had any chance of acquiring sufficient education to be able to theorize and think on the level of abstraction. Parenthetically, that was also true for men of lower classes. For millennia, the knowledge and the ability to think abstractly was monopolized by men of the upper class, eliminating men of lower class or/and subject races, and all women. In order to develop a reasoned inquiry into causes a person needs some learning, some examples of intellectual inquiry, some tools—education, in short. Only a few exceptional upper-class women throughout history have had the opportunity to acquire such knowledge.

One of the earliest of these writing in the Western World was Christine de Pisan. Typically, her argument was cast as a defense of women against the attack of literary misogynists, and in developing her argument she was forced to question the very premises on which men's arguments rested. She had to and did question men's objectivity. She exposed their self-interest in keeping women both ignorant and subject, and she challenged their religious and philosophical explanations. But before she could do that, she had to throw off the weight of male opinions and definitions; she had to conquer self-doubt. As any other woman of her day, she had been raised and educated in a culture which preached women's inferiority and equated women with evil. Attempting to answer the flood of misogynist writings, Christine de Pisan wrote in 1404: "I began to examine myself and my condition as a woman." She put her examination of her own experience and of that of other women of her day, with whom she corresponded, against the judgment and authority of men "that I might know my own judgment . . . if it were true what so many men . . . witnessed."[1] Skepticism toward handed-down doctrine is, to this day, an essential first step in raising feminist consciousness. Following Christine de Pisan there is a long tradition of learned ladies rising in defense of their sex as pamphleteers and essayists. As the historian Joan Kelly has shown, this movement, known as the *Querelles de Femmes*, is thought to have gone on for four hundred years and formed the basis of later feminist thought.[2]

Another root of feminist thought was the long tradition

---

1. Christine de Pisan, *The City of Women* (London, 1521 reprint) as cited in Joan Kelly, "Early Feminist Theory and the *Querelle des Femmes*, 1400–1789," *Signs, Journal of Women in Culture and Society* 8:1 (Autumn 1982): 9.
2. Ibid., pp. 4–28.

of female biblical criticism. The biblical tradition provided the bulk of the intellectual ammunition against women by priests, philosophers, and writers. Its argument went like this: God had created woman inferior to man; Eve was to blame for mankind's fall; St. Paul had commanded women to keep silent in the churches. The double standard of morality was sanctioned by the lives of the patriarchs: Godfather and son were representative of males; the priesthood was male and women were commanded to take doctrine, religious interpretation, and moral instruction from priests, fathers, and husbands.

One of the earliest British defenders of her sex was young Rachel Speght, a clergyman's daughter, who in 1617 answered the particularly vicious pamphlet by one Joseph Swetnam, entitled *The Arraignment of Lewd, Idle, Forward and Unconstant Women*, by publishing her own pamphlet, titled *A Mouzell for Melastomus, the Cynicall Bayter and foule mouthed Barker against Evah's Sex*.[3] She developed a spirited Bible critique, showing considerable knowledge of both the text and classical learning. She argued that woman was by God created from *refined* matter, the matter of God's own creation, while Adam had been created from dust. "She was not produced from Adam's foot to be his low inferior, nor from his head to be his superior, but from his side, near his heart, to be his equall."[4] One by one, Speght subjected the antiwoman arguments in Swetnam's tract to sharp critique and challenged the biblical interpretations in which they were grounded. Her own pamphlet and that of another woman defending her sex were published once and quickly forgotten, while Swetnam's text was republished approximately every ten years in at least eleven editions in Britain alone, the latest of them in 1807. Swetnam's pamphlet is pornographic, scatological, and generally vile and to contemplate its popularity is depressing.

At the turn of the seventeenth century, Mary Astell, one of a circle of intellectual British noblewomen, developed her own Bible critique and accused men of subjective errors in biblical translation. Hers is the first in a long line of charges made by women, that it is the translators who are to blame

---

3. Rachel Speght, *A Mouzell for Melastomus, the Cynicall Bayter and foule mouthed Barker against Evah's Sex* (London, Thos. Archer, 1617).
4. Ibid., p. 10.

for this interpretation. Astell said, they could get away with twisting the meaning of the original to their advantage because women who, without their own fault were kept in ignorance of ancient languages, could not correct them.[5] More than a century later, when the American Sarah Grimké wrote her own biblical interpretation in 1838, she arrived at similar conclusions. But because of her ignorance of women's history, Sarah Grimké, like so many women after her, did not know that others before her had reinterpreted the Bible from a feminist perspective.[6] Over and over again, individual women struggling against the weight of tradition and full of self-doubt and anxiety, had to take that difficult first step toward independent thought in isolation.

The foremost theoretician of the nineteenth-century woman's rights movement in America, Elizabeth Cady Stanton, had it a little easier in that she was initiated into such feminist ideas by another woman, Lucretia Mott. But when in the 1890s, after a lifetime spent in organizing the woman's rights movement, she published her radical feminist critique, *The Woman's Bible*, Stanton lost the support of many of her more conservative coworkers and nearly became an outcast in the movement she had helped to create.[7] She did not know then, nor did her critics, that the ideas they considered so radical in 1895 derived from a tradition of feminist Bible criticism that was two centuries old.

If the biblical foundation for the subordination of women was challenged as a wrong, another theme of feminist thought was the striving for women's education. Individual women had for centuries struggled to overcome restrictions and prejudices to acquire sound learning. But by the end of the seventeenth century, the demand of women for equal access to educational institutions was voiced in a formal way by Mary Astell, who published a plan for establishing a college for women.[8] She envisioned it as a sort of monastic in-

---

5. Mrs. Astell of Newcastle (Mary Astell) *The Christian Religion, as Profess'd by a Daughter of the Church of England* (London: R. Wilkin, 1705), p. 145.

6. Sarah Moore Grimké, *Letters on the Equality of the Sexes and the Condition of Woman* (Boston, Isaac Knapp, 1838), Letter I.

7. Elizabeth Cady Stanton, *The Woman's Bible* (New York: European Publ. Co., 1895).

8. Mary Astell, *A Serious Proposal to the Ladies, for the Advancement of their True and Greatest Interest*, 2d ed. (London, 1695).

stitution that would allow women to focus all their energies on learning. Astell secured the support, even the financial backing of noblewomen. But the plan never materialized because of strong opposition to it by the clergy. Similar ideas were proposed and voiced throughout the eighteenth century, culminating in Mary Wollstonecraft's full-fledged feminist argument, *A Vindication of the Rights of Women*.[9]

The demands for women's education became a key issue around which American women organized in the nineteenth century. Whenever individual women asserted their rights or sought to rectify a wrong, they ran into resistence. This took the form of disparagement, ridicule, economic pressure, being labeled "disobedient," and institutional barriers. It was, quite frequently, in response to such resistance that women first organized and began to experience sisterhood in practice.

Women organized in order to serve community needs. Only after they had done that did they become conscious of the need to organize for their own advancement.

In America the earliest woman's organizations were connected with the churches and usually took the form of sewing societies, the so-called "cent-societies." Women would meet weekly to sew shirts for the poor and donate a cent apiece. The money was usually used for missionary work and the training of young men to the ministry. A beautiful example of the process of coming to feminist consciousness occurred in a sewing circle in West Brookfield, Massachusetts, in 1837. The ladies, who were sewing shirts in order to support a young man through theological seminary were visited by a dynamic woman named Mary Lyon, who traveled through New England raising funds in order to found a new sort of educational institution for women. She carried a green velvet bag into which she placed the nickels, dimes, and dollars the ladies contributed and in this way raised the first $2,000 toward the foundation of Mount Holyoke Academy and later Mount Holyoke College. There was one young woman in that sewing circle who after listening to Mary Lyon concluded that "it was absurd for her to work to help educate a student who could earn more money toward his own education in a week by teaching than she could earn in a month; and she left the shirt unfinished and hoped that no

9. Mary Wollstonecraft, *A Vindication of the Rights of Woman*, 2d ed. (London: J. Johnson 1792).

one would ever complete it."[10] Her name was Lucy Stone and she became one of the great organizers of the woman's rights movement.

Women at first organized in auxiliaries to the moral reform effort of the Evangelical Ministry, in the 1830s in the cities on the eastern seaboard. The evangelical ministers were concerned about prostitution and had organized to rescue prostitutes mostly by conducting prayer services and endeavoring to persuade the prostitutes to give up their evil ways. The woman's auxiliary consisted of a group of ministers' wives, well-educated, upper-class women who were quite conservative politically and followed their husbands' lead. After a while they thought that they ought to get to know more about the life these fallen women were leading, so they began visiting the bars and the brothels. The ladies decided that a better way to prevent prostitution would be to hold prayer meetings right in front of the brothel at the time when men were entering it and in the morning, when the men were leaving. They then proceeded to take notebooks and write down the names of everyone they recognized. It had a very great effect. In fact the male reformers got quite upset about this activity and about the fact that the women were making public statements in which they referred to the prostitutes as "our sisters." So the men suggested that the ladies abandon their independent activities and rejoin the auxiliary under the leadership of the ministers, but these women said in effect, "Thank you very much, we think not and we think we will continue to have our own activity." With that they invented a new cause: to introduce laws in the legislatures that would make adultery a crime for men. They passed resolutions and circulated petitions urging women, who had always been treating the so-called "fallen woman" with contempt and banishing her from society, to treat the seducer the same way. On the basis of this new concept, which one could argue is a feminist concept, they began to organize a national movement, which spread to the Midwest and flourished in many small clubs in rural areas. The Moral Reform Societies in fact advanced an argument against the sexual double standard, but it was an argument couched in typically Victorian language. This is a beautiful example of the way in which women will take an

---

10. Alice Blackwell, *Lucy Stone* (Boston, 1930), p. 20.

activity and give it a feminist content and form, after their own experience has for a while prevailed.

Similar examples could be given of the women's antislavery organizations, which started out as auxiliaries, very soon made themselves independent, and which then became the driving force in the petitioning and organizing activities of the antislavery movement. They, in fact, did the major work of changing public opinion on the abolition issue. It was on the basis of changed public opinion that the political antislavery movement, run by men, could organize and become successful. It is typical of the state of our knowledge, that if you go to any good library today, you will find perhaps fifty books written by historians about the antislavery movement. If one takes the publishing date of 1975 as a cutoff point, one will find three books concerned with antislavery women. If one takes books published after 1975, one finds two more books about women and not a one of them that pays attention to the major activity of women, namely petitioning. That is a typical example of the way in which we have missed the meaning of women's activities. We have missed recording the activities first, and then we have missed their meaning.

Women organized great mass movements in the nineteenth century: the woman's rights conventions, later the suffrage movement, after the Civil War the vast movement of women's clubs, temperance clubs, and, in the working class the women's trade union movement. In all of these organizations women went through the necessary stages for developing feminist consciousness out of their organizing experiences.

Another route to feminist consciousness comes through the struggle of women for education. The earliest of these efforts in the U.S. is Emma Willard's Seminary in Troy, New York. In 1820, Emma Willard approached the New York legislature with a demand that a seminary, that is an academic high school for women, should be publicly funded in the same manner as boys' academies. Her request was duly considered and turned down. She then went ahead and found men and women to support her own female seminary, out of which grew a network of women, who kept in close touch with her and each other for the next fifty years and who played an important role, not only in staffing the new public school system throughout the nation, but in institution building in their own communities. A similar work was done by Catharine Beecher, in her teacher training institutions, and by Mary Lyon, in Mount Holyoke College. Later we find that as women attempt to enter professional training in graduate schools and universities, that they are excluded and forced to found sex-segregated institutions. Women's colleges, women's professional societies, the Women's Medical Association, the University Women's Association—these are all organizations founded in the process of implementing women's educational goals, running into resistance, and developing feminist consciousness. Perhaps their biggest significance was in allowing women some free space. We can visualize all of the striving of women for autonomy as struggling for space on their own terms. First, asserting that we must come in from the margin into the center and if we are blocked from coming in from the margin into the center we make our own center, create some free space, and then move into the center. That has been the process.

The third stage, defining goals and strategies autonomously—this implies a deliberate casting aside of male guidance and male forms of organization, as can be seen in the example of the Moral Reform societies. Another example occurred when the women's antislavery societies first met. The women were so timid and organizationally inexperienced that their meetings were chaired by men. A few years later, in 1837, when the first National Female Antislavery Convention met in New York City with eighty-one delegates from twelve states, the women were more self-assured. Although they had, of course, consulted with the male antislavery leadership, they refused the offer of help from, as it happened, the foremost organizer of the antislavery movement, Theodore Weld, in the following words:

> Tell Mr. Weld that when the women got together they found that they had *minds* of their own, and could transact their business *without* his direction. The Boston and Philadelphia women were so well versed in business that they were quite mortified to have Mr. Weld quoted as an authority for doing or not doing so and so.[11]

Another example of women's self-definition occurred at the Seneca Falls Convention in the debate around the demand

11. Sarah and Angelina Grimké to Theodore Weld, 18 May 1837, in *Letters of Theodore Dwight Weld, Angelina Grimké Weld and Sarah Grimké, 1822–1844*, Gilbert H. Barnes and Dwight L. Dumond, eds., 2 vols. (Gloucester, Mass.: Peter Smith, 1965 reprint of 1934 ed.) I: 388.

for woman suffrage, which was opposed by all the males present except for the great former slave Frederick Douglass. Still, the women approved it. It is also interesting to compare the resolution of the various woman's rights conventions which were held between 1848 and the Civil War with a single one of these conventions, which was entirely female, the Ohio Convention of 1850. The resolutions of the Ohio Convention are distinguished in tone from the others. They are much more self-confident. They don't apologize; they assert; they demand and they have several resolutions which condemn gender or what we would call sex role indoctrination. For example, clause 9 of the resolutions resolved:

> That the practice of holding women amenable to a different standard of propriety and morality from that to which men are held amenable, is unjust and unnatural, and highly detrimental to domestic and social virtue and happiness.[12]

Translation from Victorian: it's a double standard. At the root, the Ohio women said the double sexual standard is detrimental to women and must be abolished as a right of women.

Two other comments by nineteenth-century women indicate this coming to consciousness and to autonomy. Elizabeth Cady Stanton in her introductory remarks at the Seneca Falls Convention said the following:

> Woman herself must do this work; [of emancipation], for woman alone can understand the height, the depth, the length and the breadth of her own degradation. Man cannot speak for her, because he has been educated to believe that she differs from him so materially, that he cannot judge of her own thoughts, feelings, and opinions by his own.[13]

This was a very neat twisting of the male definition of the double standard, whereby men have said women are essentially different from us in nature. Stanton says, if we are so different from you in nature, then, kindly, let us speak for ourselves, because you don't know anything about us. And, again, Sarah Grimké on the education of women:

> Can we marvel that woman does not immediately realize the dignity of her own nature when we remember that she has

12. Reprinted from *The Emancipator*, April 1850.
13. Elizabeth Cady Stanton speech at Seneca Falls convention, 1848, as cited in Ellen DuBois, ed., *Elizabeth Cady Stanton, Susan B. Anthony, Correspondence, Writings, Speeches* (New York: Schocken Books, 1981), p. 28.

been so long used as the means to an end and that end, the comfort and pleasure of man, regarded as his property, a being created for his benefit, and living like a parasite on his vitality. When we remember how little her intellect has been taken into account in estimating her value in society, and that she received as truth the dogma of her inferiority?[14]

She says in another essay:

> Thus far woman has struggled through life with bandaged eyes, accepting the dogma of her weakness and inability to take care of herself not only physically, but intellectually.... But there is now awakened in her consciousness that she is defrauded of her legitimate Rights.... Hitherto she has surrendered her person and her individuality to man, but she can no longer do this and not feel that she is outraging her nature and her God. ... Woman ... by asserting and claiming her natural Rights, assumes the prerogative ... that she is the arbiter of her own destiny.... Self-reliance only can create true and exalted women.[15]

Finally, an alternate vision of the future. Again, some nineteenth-century examples. Most feminists at that time were concerned with altering the legal status of the married woman and fought for woman's property rights, and for woman's right to divorce, and some of them tried to keep their maiden name in marriage. Lucy Stone's name became associated with that of an organization founded to perpetuate that practice. Many of the feminists, who took their husband's names, always kept their maiden name as a middle name. A few couples, Elizabeth Cady and her husband Henry Stanton, Amelia Bloomer and her husband Dexter Bloomer, Angelina Grimké and her husband Theodore Weld, Stephen Foster and his wife Abbie Kelly Foster, a couple named Jones in Ohio, Robert Dale Owen and Emily Robinson all deliberately altered the then existing marriage contract and stated in public that the husband renounced all rights to the person and the property of his wife, which the law gave him. These were really efforts to alter existing conditions and envision a different sort of marital relationship. Later in the century, a few women took even more drastic measures.

---

14. Sarah M. Grimké, "Education of Women," Miscellaneous Essays, Weld-Grimké Papers, W. L. Clements Library, University of Michigan, Ann Arbor. Reprinted in Gerda Lerner, ed., *The Female Experience: An American Documentary* (Indianapolis: Bobbs-Merrill Co., 1977), pp. 479–80.

15. Sarah Grimké, "Sisters of Charity," ibid., p. 486.

Carrie Chapman Catt, when she entered her second marriage, made a formal contract with her husband that she would spend six months of the year being a proper wife and keeping house for him and six months of the year she would be free to travel around and organize for woman's suffrage. Which she did. Charlotte Perkins Gilman divorced her husband and kept her child with her, but found after a time that she, in her own opinion, did not make a very good mother. She decided to give the child to her husband, who had since then remarried a close friend of hers, because she thought it was better for the child and better for her. This was, at the time, considered a very shocking decision.

Another kind of expression of a vision of a different lifestyle concerns single women, who throughout the nineteenth century struggled to define a role and place for themselves that would not cast them as deviant and as objects of pity. Louisa May Alcott explained when asked why she did not marry: "I'd rather be a free woman and paddle my own canoe." This remarkable author of *Little Women* was also the author of a feminist novel. It is called *Work* and is now available in reprint.[16] It deals with the choices open to single women in her society. It describes a young girl, who leaves her grandparents' home to be independent and takes her through the drudgery jobs she is able to get. The story deals with the issue of "the fallen woman," it deals with propriety, and it deals with all the problems women face when they try to be independent. Finally, the heroine meets an unusual man, a former minister, who now runs a greenhouse. They marry, but not long after he is killed in the Civil War, leaving her pregnant. Some years later in the utopian ending of *Work* we find the heroine with her daughter living in a household, with a black woman who used to be her co-worker when she was a household worker. Also living with them are the "fallen woman," who is really a decent woman misunderstood, and an independent, poor Irish woman, who used to make her living as a washer woman. This household of women represents the utopian vision of Louisa May Alcott for single women.

The first practicing woman doctor in America, Harriot Hunt of Boston who never married, gave a great big party on what she called her twenty-fifth wedding anniversary, which was

---

16. Louisa May Alcott, *Work* (New York: Schocken Books, 1977), reprint.

actually the anniversary of the opening of her practice. Dr. Elizabeth Blackwell adopted a child and so did several other nineteenth-century professional women. In the latter part of the nineteenth century, women chose to have a life-long companionship with another woman, to have that woman be the significant other in their lives. Susan B. Anthony made a very strong statement on the subject in a speech she called "Homes of Single Women." It was one of her least popular speeches and no wonder, because it was a truly revolutionary statement for her day. She argued for the right and need of women to have homes of their own and for single women to live alone or with other women in such homes. She said:

> Even when men's intellectual convictions shall be sincerely and fully on the side of Freedom and equality to women, the force of long existing customs and laws will impel him to exert authority over her. . . . The habit of the ages cannot, at once, be changed. Not even amended constitutions and laws can revolutionize the practical relations of men and women immediately. . . . Constitutional equality . . . simply allows equality of *chances to establish equality*. Not until women shall have practically demonstrated their claim to equality in the world of work . . . [and in] politics . . . by the industry of their own hands and brains, and by election or appointment; not until they shall have actually won equality at every point morally, intellectually, physically, politically, will the superior sex really accept the fact and lay aside all assumptions, dogmatic and autocratic.
>
> Meanwhile the logic of events inevitably points to an *epoch of single women*. If women will not accept marriage with subjection, nor men proffer it without, there is, there can be no alternative. The women who will not be ruled must live without marriage. And during this transition period wherever . . . single women make comfortable and attractive homes for themselves, they furnish the best and most efficient objective lessons for men.[17]

This astonishing statement by Susan B. Anthony speaks to the striving for autonomy of a large group of educated nineteenth-century feminists.

In a later period women would also create free space in female communities within the structures of patriarchal society, which give individual women support, a sort of adop-

---

17. Susan B. Anthony, "Homes of Single Women," in DuBois, *Stanton, Anthony Correspondence*, p. 148.

tive family and freedom from the constant pressures of conforming to male dominance. Examples are the women's colleges, the settlement houses, lesbian communities at various times, and any number of utopian communities. Still we might consider this no more than utopian model building and small-scale experimental solutions to individual problems. True, but until certain preconditions have been reached and until certain levels of consciousness have been reached, no group can make practical plans for the future. All subordinate groups begin with utopian visions and only when they have reached a certain level of actual struggle and social organization can they proceed from that to a more advanced stage, the creation of a realistic program. As long as women have to constantly reinvent the wheel, individually or in small groups rediscover the process of their own self-realization, this is the level at which they will have to operate. But now we have passed an invisible threshold. Women's history enables us enormously to speed up and firm up the process of woman's emancipation. Women's Studies, especially Women's History, is the cutting edge of the feminist revolution. It validates women's experience as a basis from which to generalize and create social theory. It enables women to think of themselves and for themselves to know that there is a long tradition behind them of women doing just that, which they now can build on and no longer have to repeat. Women's Studies is not only free space for women, but a tool for shifting focus and reconstructing a vision of the world and the future in which women are no longer seen as marginal. It helps us build a vision on the premise that men and women always have and will in the future share the world, the world's work and the ideas which help us to order the world. It means placing women at the center, not only of events, where we have always been, but of the thinking work of the world. Women thinking for themselves must overcome the need for male approval.

We must learn to trust our own experience and the judgment of other women. Feminist consciousness, historically slow in coming into being, presupposes a constant testing of thought in action, a constant reinforcement of generalizations by particular experience. It inevitably leads to a social transformation, since its very coming into being is a challenge to a world which has for millennia been so defined as to make women appear marginal. But because civilization has been built by men and women, women have throughout historical times been excluded from the creation of symbol-systems, while all the time they have been sharing with men the work of the world and the building of civilization. The causes of this sexual inequality are ancient and complex. They are not God given, they are not natural, they are historically determined. The various factors that thousands of years ago made such a sexual division of labor necessary have long been superceded. Women, as well educated as men, are challenging the one-sided view of life and the world, which our androcentric civilization offers us as absolute truth. We are saying that our side of the truth has not been told and now must be told. Our historical experience must no longer remain unrecorded and our talents must no longer be predetermined as being suitable for one kind of activity rather than for another, solely because of our sex. For women, education has traditionally meant learning to enter a world of intellectual constructs made by men, expressed in symbols controlled by men, and arranged in systems and frameworks to the creation of which women were marginal. For women students, becoming educated has first and foremost meant learning to think like men and to aspire to the goals and modes of living a professionalism formed by men. Today, educated women and women students are challenging this process and demanding as man did in the Renaissance, the right to be at the center of the human enterprise—the right to define, the right to decide. Women are asking for self-definition and autonomy. This means a paradigm shift. Women are challenging educators to end the distorted, one-sided view of civilization and history academies have called universal. A thorough transformation of curricula, of approaches, of attitudes is needed in order to bring the by now larger half of our student body away from marginality into the center of our educational enterprise. The task is enormous, the challenge is inevitable and will not fade away. Intellectually, the process is revitalizing and invigorating. Women's Studies is the cutting edge of a cultural transformation which will enrich the intellectual and actual lives of men and women now and in the future. But above all, Women's History is Woman's Right.

Nancy Walker and Bobbie Burk, co-chairs of the Symposium Planning Committee.

Nancy Walker

The Effects of Social Change on the Lives of Women
Summary, Session 1

Gerda Lerner's talk, "The Rise of Feminist Consciousness," provided both a historical framework and a set of definitions that became reference points for the succeeding sessions of the symposium. Following upon Patricia Graham's keynote address the evening before, which had identified broad changes in the relationship of women to education and to society, participants in this first topical session began to narrow the focus of the symposium to specific issues in the future of women's education. Lerner's insistence that women know their own history so that they do not work in isolation for equality was reinforced by the two panelists who responded to Lerner's remarks and by the question-and-answer session that followed. One dominant theme emerging from this session was the necessity to free women from the mythologies surrounding them—both presuppositions about woman's capacity for nurturance and avoidance of technology and media-inspired ideas of "superwoman" and the "post-feminist generation."

The first panelist responding to Lerner's talk, William Chafe, professor of history at Duke University, directed his remarks to the social realities of women's and men's lives in the present, especially the disparity between private efforts for equality and public policies that undermine those efforts. Pointing to women's increased determination to make changes in their lives—the movement from awareness to self-definition to which Lerner had pointed—Chafe stressed the need for women simultaneously to question the assumptions and values of a society that rewards single-minded devotion to a professional life instead of systematically providing day care for children and flexible working hours for both women and men to allow for mutual family responsibilities and equal access to professional achievement. Chafe's central point was that the private and public spheres are intimately related, so that the individual must influence public policy in order to be able to make personal choices about career and family. For women truly to exercise choice about their private lives would require "a radical transformation in the entire structure of values, institutions, and assumptions of the society"—the "alternate vision of the future" that Lerner had identified as the fourth stage in the movement toward woman's emancipation.

Jo Hartley, founder and editor of *Comment*, followed Chafe by presenting a more optimistic view of women's ability to influence social change. Though acknowledging that sexism is still a potent force, Hartley pointed to women's increased political involvement in specific efforts such as promoting the Equal Rights Amendment and, more generally, in voting patterns during recent years. Hartley stressed, however, that since only 27 percent of women can be identified as full-time homemakers, employment trends bear watching, and the change from the industrial to the information society will require women to become more comfortable with computer and other technology.

The issues raised during the ensuing question-and-answer period centered on woman's nurturant abilities versus her current tendency to assume a masculine identity in the work place, factors affecting women's status both in marriage and in jobs, and the threat to equality posed by the priorities of the New Right and the so-called "post-feminist generation." In response to a question about men and women as subcategories of humanity, Lerner urged that we cease to think of the world as "divisible between men and women," but instead work for a "feminist transformation" to create a society based on a "joint image of the world." One concern voiced many times during the symposium was the extent to which women's physiological differences are viewed as negative rather than positive—e.g., woman's ability to bear children becomes a barrier to her fulfillment and contribution in other areas of life, and therefore women wish to deny this part of their capability. Lerner pointed out the societal double bind in which women find themselves: relegated to a lower status than men precisely because of their childbearing function and then unable to have significant careers in midlife because of the years spent in nurturing the young. Calling herself an "eternalist," Lerner proposed that greater value be placed on nurturance by both women and men and reminded the participants that in an age which has the potential for nuclear war, the entire planet is in need of the nurturing relationship that has been perceived as existing only between mother and child. In terms of education, Lerner suggested that all students must be aware of the long tradition of reform and benevolence in America that has been the product of both male and female altruism, and stated that the "biggest argument for feminism" is its potential "redefinition of community on a global scale."

Lerner and Chafe succeeded in creating a sense of community among the symposium participants with their remarks about the New Right and the "post-feminist generation." Several questions reflected concern that the agenda of the Moral Majority and apparent political apathy on the part of the college generation signaled a retreat from the commitment to equality. Chafe maintained that it would be a mistake to overemphasize the impact of the New Right, because in doing so we might let others decide what the issues are. The 1980 elections did not realign American politics except in the view of those who wished that to be true; the task, he said, is to continue to work for human rights both inside and outside the academy. Lerner concurred, adding that the significance of a social movement may in part be measured by the opposition it arouses. Bringing the session full circle to women's history, Lerner insisted that the much-touted "post-feminist generation" was a media creation based on scant evidence. She preferred to speak of a "lag in feminist consciousness"—a lack of awareness on the part of young women that those before them had struggled for the gains they now take for granted, and a concomitant desire to succeed individually without helping other women along. Insisting that knowledge of women's history is an effective way of resisting social forces that work against equality, Lerner concluded, "We have a very fine heritage. We are not starting from nothing. We didn't invent [the women's movement] in 1970, and we have a tradition that we can be proud of and that we must pass on."

Patricia Bell Scott

Education for Self-Empowerment: A Priority for Women of Color

Though historical records are sparse, the evidence suggests that attempts by women of color to obtain quality education have been thwarted by American mores and values, prejudice against women, and racial discrimination.[1] By women of color I mean black, Hispanic, Asian, and Native-American women, labels I use reluctantly because using them has resulted in an under-appreciation of the diversity within it. Black can also refer to Puerto Rican, Cuban, or Jamaican. The Asian label refers to many—some Chinese, some Japanese, others Filipino. Many different tribes are grouped under the category of Native-American or American Indian. Of this label Owanah Anderson, founder and director, Ohoyo Resource Center, has remarked, "Many years ago, when I was a child, my grandmother used to say to me, 'If anyone asks if you are Indian . . . you tell them no. You tell them you're Choctaw.'"[2] This diversity is indicative of how different our voices are and illustrates that within each ethnic group are many cultural variances. Yet, all women of color share the burdens of race and sex prejudice—prejudices so deep as to be taken for granted, like the air we breathe—even within our own communities.

The question of how women of color would be educated

1. See *La Chicana: Building for the Future an Action Plan for the 80's* (Oakland, Calif.: The National Hispanic University, 1981); *Journal of Negro Education* (special issue on "The Impact of Black Women in Education") 51:3 (Summer 1982); C. Moraga and G. Anzaldua, *This Bridge Called My Back: Writings by Radical Women of Color*; *Ohoyo Ikhana: A Bibliography of American Indian-Alaska Native Curriculum Materials* (Wichita Falls, Texas: Ohoyo Resource Center, 1982).

2. Ohoyo Resource Center, *Words of Today's American Indian Women: Ohoyo Makachi* (Wichita Falls, Texas: Ohoyo Resource Center, 1982).

Speaker Patricia Bell Scott talks with respondent Fontaine Belford after the session on the special needs of women in higher education.

has been broached with contempt or fear. After all, why should a society dominated and ruled by non-minority males expend its resources to educate the second-class citizens—namely the females—of second-class racial and cultural ethnic groups?

We have been victims of social attitudes about the "proper place" of women. For this reason we have been subject to the pressures most women face in educational institutions—the pressure to educate one's self for motherhood, homemaking, or perhaps some "nurturing" professional role, such as nursing, social work, or teaching.

People of color have been victims of the negative stereotypes about the intellectual abilities of nonwhites. Since nonwhites are supposed to be incapable of great intellectual rigor—why should anyone expect the weaker sex of a weak group to be capable of serious scholarship? The prevailing attitude about the education of nonwhite women has been that we are only capable of (and should be trained for) work without intellectual challenge and work that enhances our moral character.

The view of Alexander Crummell on the education of black girls in 1891 reflects a theme common to beliefs about the education of women of color generally:

> Let us state here definitely what I want for the black girls of the South. . . . I wish the intellectual training . . . limited to reading, writing, arithmetic and geography . . . they should be taught accurately all domestic work.[3]

That Crummell was a respected black educator reflects the extent to which sexism is ingrained in the psyche of our own communities.

Because most of us have been subject to some kind of slavery, we have been thought to be in special need of educational experiences that promote moral character. Many educators—colored and otherwise—have stressed Christian education and advised strict discipline for colored women students. In her 1978 book on black women's history, Jeanne Noble wrote about the fear that has shaped the education of black women:

> There is a fear that the Black woman would revert to the sins of her mother—become a concubine. . . . And education, above

3. A. Crummell, *Africa and America* (Springfield, Mass.: Wiley and Co., 1891), p. 80.

all else, was to keep her a virgin, give her a practical way to make a living.[4]

I argue that this fear remains with us and that women of color grow into womanhood in a milieu where the classical liberal education is viewed as dangerous. Education has been circumscribed according to racist and sexist traditions; access to it has been limited and participation in educational experiences not traditional for our ethnic groups has been prohibited. So it is against this sociocultural backdrop that the contemporary picture emerges.

A Profile

At the beginning of this decade, the statistical profile for women of color indicates that:
- we make up more than half the population of our respective ethnic groups,
- we are urban dwellers—with more than half of us living in central cities,
- we are a young group with considerable longevity—the median age is 25.2 and the life expectancy is 72.6 years,
- we head alone the majority of nonwhite families living in poverty,
- we are more likely than white women to experience family dissolution,
- we have families that are slightly larger than our white counterparts,
- we represent a rapidly increasing proportion of women who never marry,
- we have historically (and continue to have) high participation in the labor force, where we work largely in white-collar jobs as clerical workers and in blue-collar jobs as service workers,
- we earn a median income slightly less than white women but significantly less than white and colored men, and
- we are more likely to be the victims of violent crimes.[5]

4. J. Noble, *Beautiful Also, Are the Souls of My Black Sisters: A History of the Black Woman in America.*
5. *A Statistical Portrait of Women in the United States: 1978,* current population reports (special studies, series P-23, no. 100). Bureau of the Census (Washington, D.C.: U.S. Government Printing Office, 1980).

There are some differences among us which are important to point out. For example, Native-Americans have less education than any group of women, live primarily in rural areas (some 20 percent on reservations), are considerably younger than all women, and have the lowest median income of any group. Japanese, Chinese, and Filipino women are slightly older than women generally, have lower birth rates, and are more likely to be white-collar and professional workers. Cuban, Puerto Rican, and Chicano women are slightly younger than women generally and represent the fastest-growing segment of the American minority population.[6]

This profile suggests that we represent a sizeable group of young, poor learners, who live in urban settings besieged with economic woes that cripple the educational systems serving us. Though we have moved into the world of white- and blue-collar workers in significant numbers, we are occupationally segregated in low-paying jobs. Our longevity, the present economic depression, and the pressures of race and sex discrimination contribute to the likelihood that many of us will head families alone. In summary, we are in dire need of educational and occupational experiences that elevate our life circumstances.

The Contemporary Scene: Myths and Stereotypes

Like our foremothers, our educational experiences are clouded by myths about the purpose of education for women and stereotypes of people of color. Though it is generally believed that education provides a route "out of the ghetto," that has not always been the case for us. In general, the educational preparation we receive prepares us for work in the female worlds of nursing, teaching, and social work. We typically take whatever skills we develop back to our communities or to segregated arenas with other women professionals in the larger society.

It is only recently that researchers have begun to ask us how we feel about the quality of our education. Though the data are scant, some insights have emerged. For example, autobiographical accounts reveal that women of color describe being educated "away from ourselves,"[7] that the

6. Ibid.
7. See Gloria T. Hull, Patrica Bell Scott, and Barbara Smith, eds., *All the Women Are White, All the Blacks Are Men, But Some of Us Are Brave: Black*

educational process does not reinforce one's identity. Because the educational process begins long before formal schooling, the impact on identity and self-esteem is profound. The poem, "When I Was Growing Up," by Nellie Wong, a Chinese-American writer and union organizer, best illustrates this point.

> I know now that once I longed to be white.
> How? you ask.
> Let me tell you the ways.
>   when I was growing up, people told me
> I was dark and I believed my own darkness
>   in the mirror, in my soul, my own narrow vision
>   when I was growing up, my sisters
>   with fair skin got praised
>   for their beauty, and in the dark
>   I fell further, crushed between high walls
> when I was growing up, I read magazines
> and saw movies, blonde movie stars, white skin,
> sensuous lips and to be elevated, to become
> a woman, a desirable woman, I began to wear
> imaginary pale skin
>   when I was growing up, I was proud
>   of my English, my grammar, my spelling
>   fitting into the group of smart children
>   smart Chinese children, fitting in,
>   belonging, getting in line
> when I was growing up and went to high school,
> I discovered the rich white girls, a few yellow girls,
> their imported cotton dresses, their cashmere sweaters,
> their curly hair and I thought that I too should have
> what these lucky girls had
>   when I was growing up, I hungered
>   for American food, American styles,
>   coded: white and even to me, a child
>   born of Chinese parents, being Chinese
>   was feeling foreign, was limiting,
>   was unAmerican
> when I was growing up and a white man wanted
> to take me out, I thought I was special,
> an exotic gardenia, anxious to fit
> the stereotype of an oriental chick
>   when I was growing up, I felt ashamed

Women's Studies; Cherrie Moraga and Gloria Anzaldua, *This Bridge Called My Back*; M. Terrell, A *Colored Woman in a White World* (Washington, D.C.: Randsdell Publishing Co., 1940).

> of some yellow men, their small bones,
> their frail bodies, their spitting
> on the streets, their coughing,
> their lying in sunless rooms,
> shooting themselves in the arms
>
> when I was growing up, people would ask
> if I were Filipino, Polynesian, Portuguese.
> They named all colors except white, the shell
> of my soul, but not my dark, rough skin
>
> when I was growing up, I felt
> dirty. I thought that god
> made white people clean
> and no matter how much I bathed,
> I could not change, I could not shed
> my skin in the gray water
>
> when I was growing up, I swore
> I would run away to purple mountains,
> houses by the sea with nothing over
> my head, with space to breathe,
> uncongested with yellow people in an area
> called Chinatown, in an area I later learned
> was a ghetto, one of many hearts
> of Asian America
>
> I know now that once I longed to be white.
> How many more ways? you ask.
> Haven't I told you enough?[8]

Women of color, like women and colored men generally, find the classroom environment chilly and unreceptive to those who are bright. There is some indication that capable women of color do not perform as they could. In *Nappy Edges*, Ntozake Shange talks about what it's like to be talented, black and ignored:

> . . . be a smart child trying to be dumb . . .
> not blk enuf to lovinly ignore . . .
> not bitter enuf to die at a early age . . .[9]

Sarah Lightfoot in her work on the opposing worlds of schools and minority families makes the following observation of a young black girl, Jackie:

> Why is it that Jackie, an aggressive, domineering, expressive, and bright-eyed dark-skinned girl becomes lethargic, accom-

---

8. N. Wong, "When I Was Growing Up," In C. Moraga and G. Anzaldua, eds., *This Bridge Called My Back*, p. 7.
9. N. Shange, *Nappy Edges*.

modating, mask-wearing, shadowy figure in school? Why is she so visible, so colorful, so skillful skipping rope with her friends on the street, so responsible, so bossy, so nurturant with her younger brothers and sisters; and why do these striking qualities vanish in school?[10]

I personally will never forget my first year as a college student at a large, predominantly white university in 1968. I was part of "an experiment" that year; about one hundred black freshmen entered a university community of thirty thousand white students. I will remember always my excitement at moving into my dorm room—my first day at chemistry lab—meeting my lab partner, a white male, destined to be a doctor, so he said. I was astonished at how average he was. In fact, he was what I had learned to call "barely above dumb." And yet I remember how much encouragement he received from the professor, and how much surprise my A scores on tests elicited from the same professor. I received no reinforcement for my excellent performance. This experience was made more difficult by the fact that I had no one with whom to share these discoveries and anxieties. I eventually learned to accept rejection and not to expect encouragement from anyone except parents for good work. I came to believe that academic success was something I had to achieve in spite of the classroom environment. Needless to say, I could have been a better, more creative student had the reinforcements been there.

Despite the blossoming of Black Studies, Chicano Studies, Native-American Studies, and Women's Studies, my work suggests that women of color are still being educated away from themselves. The incentive for compiling the book, *All the Women Are White, All the Blacks Are Men, But Some of Us Are Brave: Black Women's Studies*, was to provide a tool that would help integrate content on black women into Women's Studies and Black Studies programs. One of my biggest concerns is that Women's Studies as a field will come to mirror white male studies—that it will be racist, classist, and homophobic. Unfortunately, few introductory courses in Women's Studies really reflect the experiences of women

10. Sarah L. Lightfoot, "Young Black Girls: the Separate Worlds of Families and Schools," in *Proceedings of Symposium on the Socialization of Black Women* (Washington, D.C.: National Advisory Council on Women's Educational Programs, 1979).

as a group. The growing number of curriculum materials on women of color makes the argument that there is no scholarship or literature in this area an empty one.[11]

As people who are committed to women's education, it behooves us to learn and teach what we know about our common differences. Since women and people of color should be prepared to run the societies on this planet in the next two decades, it is imperative that we design educational curricula that reinforce who we are and teach us how to be more human.

Educational Priorities for the 1980s

Our history and the contemporary scene reveal the following educational priorities for the 1980s:
- a need to keep access at the top of the list of educational equity issues,
- a need for diverse and creative strategies for financing our education,
- a need to support scholarship on women of color—scholarship that will change the knowledge base of the traditional curriculum,
- a need for career counseling, mentoring relationships, networks, and role models to enhance the educational experience,
- a need for occupational job-training programs designed to prepare us for the workplace of the future, and
- a need to see and have more women of color as leaders and policymakers in all spheres of American life.

Obviously, the fight against economic discrimination and race and sex prejudice is central to the accomplishment of these priorities. Though small, the list of resource groups committed to the struggle is growing.[12]

In summary, the educational needs of women of color

11. See Hull, Bell Scott, and Smith, *But Some of Us Are Brave*; Moraga and Anzaldua, *This Bridge Called My Back*; Patricia Bell Scott, *A Basic Resource List of Places Where Curriculum Development on Women of Color Is Done and Disseminated*, available from the author at 38 Holiday Street, Dorchester, MA 02122.

12. See resources listed in Hull, Bell Scott, and Smith, *But Some of Us Are Brave*; Moraga and Anzaldua, *This Bridge Called My Back*; and Bell Scott, *A Basic Resource List*.

have not changed substantially over the past century. Access to formal schooling is still a problem, and the quality and appropriateness of our educational experiences are often of a questionable nature. It is my hope that this paper will serve as a catalyst in the struggle for educational equity.

I would like to leave you with a poem, somewhat frustrating in tone, yet very real. It is my favorite poem and though it is written from the perspective of a black woman, it represents an experience unique to and common among women of color. It's called "The Bridge Poem" by Donna Kate Rushin. In this poem, she talks about the way in which women of color are a bridge between minority communities and the community of women. She talks about the need for self-empowerment—and that can only come about with recognition and understanding of our place in the world community. She writes:

> I've had enough
> Im sick of seeing and touching
> Both sides of things
> Sick of being the damn bridge for everybody
>
> Nobody
> Can talk to anybody
> Without me
> Right?
>
> I explain my mother to my father my father to my little sister
> My little sister to my brother my brother to the white feminists
> The white feminists to the Black church folks the Black church
>   folks
> To the ex-hippies the ex-hippies to the Black separatists the
> Black separatists to the artists the artists to my friends'
>   parents. . .
>
> Then
> Ive got to explain my self
> To everybody
>
> I do more translating
> Than the Gawdamn U.N.
>
> Forget it
> I'm sick of it
>
> I'm sick of filling in your gaps
>
> Sick of being your insurance against
> The isolation of your self-imposed limitations

Sick of being the crazy at your holiday dinners
Sick of being the odd one at your Sunday Brunches
Sick of being the sole Black friend to 34 individual white people

Find another connection to the rest of the world
Find something else to make you legitimate
Find some other way to be political and hip

I will not be the bridge to your womanhood
Your manhood
Your human-ness

I'm sick of reminding you not to
Close off too tight for too long

I'm sick of mediating with your worst self
On behalf of your better selves

I am sick
Of having to remind you
To breathe
Before you suffocate
Your own fool self

Forget it
Stretch or drown
Evolve or die
The bridge I must be
Is the bridge to my own power
I must translate
My own fears
Mediate
My own weaknesses

I must be the bridge to nowhere
But my true self
And then
I will be useful[13]

Let us all commit ourselves to building educational institutions and experiences that promote the self-empowerment of women of color. For the strength of women of color is crucial to us all.

13. D. Rushin, "The Bridge Poem." In Moraga and Anzaldua, *This Bridge Called My Back*, p. xxi.

Cynthia Secor and Carolyn Dorsey respond to questions from the audience.

Bernice Williamson

Special Needs of Women
Summary, Session 2

Fontaine Belford presented a philosophical approach to understanding women's needs and the reasons for the lack of concern for these needs in education. In her view, the analysis of this "mind set" is now resulting in a major transformation in an educational system that heretofore has not responded to the requirements of women. Belford spoke of the influence of language on what people know and the world they know. Educational systems are organized with the idea of transmitting a given set of values. Thus, the disciplines include certain views and exclude others. The world people see is an "invention of language." They cannot see the whole. Perceptions, influenced by language, are partial. Individuals look at their world or their spaces through particular categories, i.e., white is good, black is bad.

How a person thinks is related to what she/he thinks. Because of these thought patterns, individuals differ in their analysis of problems and the decisions they make on what to include or exclude in looking at such issues as the special needs of women: "Our method of structuring our thought doesn't describe something; it tells us something. What it tells us is that it is not and has not been describing what women have been trying to think." Belford also noted that basic to her statement of women's special needs is that "no truth can be accepted as final . . . every experience and its codification has to be subject to revision."

Studies have documented the fact that women who graduate from women's colleges achieve professional success more frequently than do women graduates of coeducational schools. However, Belford questioned whether the curriculum in most women's colleges is different than that in men's colleges; women are simply educated separately from men. This point was challenged during the discussion period for this session, and Belford noted some exceptions to this fact.

Belford raised several questions: Do people have the right to shape their education to their needs? Are women in their urge to succeed giving up the "luxury to pour energy into what is rather than what one does?" Women should not have to stay home, cook and sew and look after the children. But is anyone training men to do it? She concluded, "Where does all of this lead us? It leads us many places. Basic to all of this is the transformation of education and of the educational process."

In her opening statement, Helen Astin referred to Patricia Graham's comments on the qualities frequently believed to be of importance to young women of the 1980s. She should be "attractive, active, ambitious, and ambivalent." Astin emphasized ambition and ambivalence. She characterized ambivalence as "searching for a solution. . . . We do not stay with the same values. . . . we examine what we mean by being ambitious." The achievement orientation of students is of particular concern in light of efforts to transform education and society. National studies in which Astin has been engaged since 1966 have identified significant goal changes for students. They have moved from humanitarian, social-political values to materialistic "I," "Me" values.

These changes are especially apparent in women. According to Astin, women are saying the only way to make it is to incorporate the materialistic values. Women are making very traditional career choices in spite of the fact that many of them profess an interest in medicine and law. A 1980 study of college women indicated they were either in traditional fields or training for entry into them.

While different groups of women have different agendas, all college women have three needs: 1) to prepare for gainful employment; 2) to re-examine their values and restructure them; 3) to develop a sense of confidence and well-being. The question is, how do educators facilitate the student's development? Also, what experiences can college women have that will "enhance their sense of self-worth?" And, what makes it possible for young women to pursue nontraditional areas of study and persist in "new fields of inquiry"? Data demonstrate that higher education can provide leadership opportunities and experiences in sports that have a powerful influence on feelings of competence and self-worth.

Faculty values have an impact on students. According to some studies, in a research-oriented institution faculty who interacted with students and treated them as colleagues in an enterprise provided students with a great sense of self-esteem. Previously, this type of interaction has been reserved for men. The aspirations of college women have changed since 1966. Now women are more likely to want to be recognized as authorities in their fields, to develop administrative skills, and to achieve success. A smaller number are interested in producing works of art, becoming involved in environmental issues, or engaging in community action.

More research is needed to understand the nature of ambition. Astin expressed the hope that women will enter the traditionally male fields, but in so doing they will bring their nurturing values with them. She stated, "I would like those corporations to be conformed to us rather than for us to transform ourselves to enter them."

The discussion following panelists Belford and Astin centered around issues regarding the needs of women of color. A student from Smith College asked Pat Bell Scott, "How do we prevent the sense that black women need to assimilate to achieve." Scott responded that black students at predominately white colleges congregate in groups in order to seek a sense of camaraderie with people like themselves. Once they are comfortable with their environment, they move into other spheres of the campus community. The basic underlying need is the need to recognize and appreciate the ways in which people are different. Scott urged students to talk about "common differences" in formal settings so that these discussions can filter down to informal discussions.

According to Scott, "the biggest struggle for a black woman age eighteen to twenty-one is to make it through the environment and come out feeling good about herself. When this is added to the task of functioning as a student leader and doing well academically, you realize this is quite a task." Fontaine Belford added, "Separate is not as much a threat as togetherness unless it is enforced by other people."

Nancy Barcelo, an administrator at the University of Iowa, stated that many minorities feel they have to assimilate to succeed. She spoke to the necessity for a strong sense of cultural identity. She referred to studies that show that Mexican women experiencing the highest attrition from college enrollment are those who are assimilating. Students who are proud of being Chicano are making it.

Gerda Lerner added a global perspective to this discussion. She suggested that every white man and white woman involved in American education today should be concerned with the fact that they are being trained to live in a world that is predominately not white: "Power is shifting from the industrial nations to the Third World, a term that is absurd because it assumes there is something first that is white." The discussion came to a close with a reformed view of the golden rule. Pat Bell Scott reiterated the need "to go beyond trying to treat people like we would like to be treated because everyone is not like us."

Elizabeth Kamarck Minnich

From Fate to Inheritance

The curriculum in our institutions of higher education is not now designed adequately to support our women students in becoming strong, independent, resourceful, creative, and successful adults. What we are teaching at present, how we are teaching it, and the setting in which the learning is supposed to take place tend to contradict our own stated goals. If we changed nothing but helped our students develop a strong sense of irony, we would have taken a real step toward strengthening also their sense of themselves, but we don't usually approach our own campuses ironically (however skillfully we may find the ironies in the approaches of others). Our students—all of them but particularly the non-minority students (women, black men, et al.)—are left with a preconscious sense of discrepancy, and too often they feel the discrepancy between themselves and the world of achievement, rather than between our stated purposes and what we are, in fact, teaching.

The gap between mission and practice is ironical and not hypocritical. It is not individual or institutional purposes that are at issue here: It is a set of discrepancies worked into our tradition so thoroughly that we are all caught by them. Our very language reflects as it continues to shape that tradition, of course, and our meaning systems, and our political, social, economic, legal systems. Yet at present, despite the vast outpouring of feminist scholarship that is in direct response to the need to carry out a critique of the minority tradition, we are used to calling "ours," most of us do not teach a critical, reflexive view of all that we have inherited. Hannah Arendt once said that if we do not know our history

At a workshop session, Elizabeth Kamarck Minnich emphasizes the need for a revised and refocused liberal education that is more empowering for women. To her left is Barbara Losty, workshop chair.

(and not just that written in books but that embedded in our meaning systems as a whole), we are doomed to live it as if it were our own private fate.[1] The feminist slogan, "The personal is the political," reflects a similar awareness of the need to uncover what has been covered up so that we do not each suffer as if it were our own what is a dominant aspect of the world we all share.

What, then, are some of these discrepancies in our tradition?

The simplest and most far-reaching expression is the oft-repeated determination—it's not a statement, it's a determination—that *he*, *man*, *mankind* are generic terms. The issue surrounding the use of the male pronoun has, incidentally, provoked an inordinate amount of scorn. It is perceived by many as a trivial issue. But what seems trivial seems so precisely because it is common, everyday, all pervasive, unchallenged. And that is exactly where we ought to expect to find the deepest assumptions of our culture, not just in the sophisticated texts, the books and works created by the few for the few.

Man simply does not, in fact, include everybody. We make our first mistake by taking an abstract, singular term as the universal. Immediately, we have left out of account human plurality and diversity. If we start with *man* or *mankind* (any singular *kind*), we are going to have to add on considerations of difference. How, then, are we going to think about all of us without constantly fighting something we have already built into the foundations of our thinking, the assumption that what is most basic, most important is what is like rather than unlike about us. Difference becomes, at best, a problem for us. It is a problem in our culture.

Secondly, and relatedly, some human differences were, from the beginning of our tradition (by which I mean the dominant Euro-American tradition) actually not ignored at all. They were considered to disqualify most of us from being fully human. Gender differences are the prime case. The few men who were privileged to lead lives of leisure that allowed for learning and scholarship (the word *scholar* itself derives from the word for leisure, skholázein) considered

---

1. Hannah Arendt, *Rachel Varnhagen: The Life of a Jewish Woman*, rev. ed. (New York: Harcourt, Brace, Jovanovich, 1974).

most other kinds of lives not fully human. And those kinds of lives were the lives into which all women, as well as male slaves, and male workers, were forced. Right there at the beginning we see a model of circular thinking, precisely the kind that has created such havoc for us through the ages. Aristotle argued that people who are slaves lead slavelike lives, lives subject to necessity and therefore less than fully human, and are by that fact proven to be slavish by nature. He argues in a similar vein for the "natural" inferiority of women. These passages of Aristotle, who was called simply The Philosopher for the centuries during which the dominant tradition was developing, cannot be ignored as if they had no implications for the rest of this thinking either. If all that Aristotle says about "man" and "mankind" is read as if it pertains to all of us, it is being misread.[2]

Aristotle is only one example, of course, albeit an inordinately influential one. Read almost any of the "great works" of the dominant traditions thoroughly and in the complete context of the author's thought and you will find that *he* and *man* and *mankind* are not intended to apply to women, slaves, and laboring people in general. Most of humanity was intentionally omitted from the terms most basic to the canon we now take to be our tradition, not only because of the singularity of the term *man* but also because *man* was defined in distinction from—often in opposition to—all those other human sorts who were not allowed to live lives worthy of *a man*. This tradition is the one being passed on in our universities, our own personal good intentions notwithstanding. *Mankind* is a purposefully partial term, in both senses of *partial*.

We have not pointed that out to our students, despite the fact that it is part of almost all the books we teach and the subjects we study. At best we have dissociated ourselves from the prejudices of thinkers like Aristotle (and Augustine and Thomas and Freud and Tolstoy and Kant and John Adams . . .), feeling free, then, to teach these great thinkers as pillars of our tradition. But, of course, what happens then is that we leave our students with a view of humanity that omits the lives, achievements, values, contributions, struggles,

2. Aristotle presents woman as intermediate between man and beast in many of his works, one of them is "Politics, 1252a–1252b," in *The Basic Works of Aristotle*, R. McKeon, ed. (New York: Random House, 1941).

and beauty of the majority of humankind in favor of a partial view that claims universality.

There is the heart of the irony we build into our students as we have it deep in our own hearts and minds and sense of self. Take the vivid example of the by-now classic Broverman study, in which psychologists, psychiatrists, and social workers were asked to describe a normal human, a normal man, and a normal woman. They described a normal human and a normal man in the same terms, and a normal woman in different terms.[3] Women and nonprivileged men were defined as different from *man*, yet *man* was defined as *human*. *Man* is not only partial, it is normative and oppositional (it excludes the majority).

We know the cost of that kind of conceptual error. It skews all further thinking because the part cannot be simultaneously the whole. And that skewed thinking informs our lives. The notions about qualities of greatness that we teach women do not coincide with what we are also taught in the practice of daily life about what it means to be a "normal" woman. A vivid example of the cost of that discrepancy is in the fate of too many "good girls," good women, whose trained and enforced dependence on men prepares them very poorly for independence that is often forced on them in a still unfair world. Increasingly, women are the majority of the nation's poor. Even our young, affluent white men can suffer from a sense of discrepancy between themselves and the models of greatness presented in what we teach because we so rarely teach works in their context (we are so stuck on the singularity of man that we do not show what it really takes to be great—all the others on whom greatness relies). But our young women are in a worse position, of course: Even if the singular models of greatness were in context, still the great exclude us. They are, these models that dot our curriculum, in fact, men, and if we know nothing else, we know that women are not men, and that we must not try to be like men. That leaves us with nothing but notions of greatness that we are not to emulate, in a context in which we are being told (explicitly or implicitly) that these are our models, that we are included. Confusing, no?

3. Inge K. Broverman et al., "Sex-Role Stereotypes and Clinical Judgments of Mental Health," *Journal of Consulting and Clinical Psychology* 34 (1970): 1–7.

So, there is the discrepancy between *man* and any concept that would take account of, rather than make a problem of, diversity. There is the discrepancy between *man* and *human* that persists in the face of our claims that all are included precisely because each half of humanity is simultaneously taught that men and women are quite, quite different and ought to be so. There is the discrepancy between our models of greatness and the realities of any students' lives, since we live perforce in contexts but our great works are usually taught out of any but a scholarly context, exacerbated unbearably for women who are given no models or contexts at all that we are in fact allowed to see as our own. And let me add that women, like other not-quite-human creatures according to the dominant tradition, have indeed been allowed on occasion to be exceptions but that an exception not only experiences discrepancy but in fact is a discrepancy. An exceptional man is one who stands out among his kind. An exceptional woman either stands out among a kind whch is not *mankind*, and therefore does not fit into the notions of importance and greatness of the tradition taught in our schools, or stands out as other than her kind, yet not of mankind, either. Surely it is destructive that a woman, according to the world as seen in our curricula, can only be outstanding in the terms of that tradition if she ceases to be like other women, ceases to be what in fact she is while not becoming what in fact she is not, a man. Being recognized as exceptional would seem to be good, but it twists on us, and in us. It leaves us with nowhere to stand, no one to stand with. While most of these ideas about the dominant tradition are familiar territory to most of us, they are essential in a consideration of how the curriculum, and the hidden curriculum, in our schools can change in order to help strengthen our students for their futures.

It ought to be quite clear by now that adding anything on to the curriculum can only help a bit, but that every little bit is, in fact, very important. I do not want to argue that the additive approach is wrong; I do want to argue that what we are engaged in as we carry out a feminist critique of the liberal arts tradition and the institutions that claim to carry it on is much more basic than any of us realized when we started thinking about it all. We are trying to bring wholeness and diversity to a partial singular tradition. It is that simple, and that difficult. Intellectually, there is a need to review all our key terms, constructs, theories, models to check their claims to generality, let alone universality. Where scholars have been careful to delimit their terms as to the historical period, the class, the culture, the sample size—whatever kind of delimitation emerges in the different fields—we need to ask if they also are open about their gender limitations. We need to do that as scholars, so that our own work can be accurate. We also need to do it as teachers, so that our students learn, with us, that truth matters more than the preservation of old prejudices enshrined, as they are, in "masterpieces" or hidden behind inadequately examined "objectivity." If we change nothing in what we teach, but simply begin asking the questions, "Does that apply to women, too?" and "Was it in fact intended to?" we will have taken a major step. And we will have begun better serving not only truth but also our students. These simple questions tell women as well as men studying with us that it matters whether well over half the human race is included. And they help make explicit the question all young people ask themselves as they work with us: Does it matter, what I am studying? These days that question tends to be interpreted as career-oriented. "Does it matter?" means "Will it help me get a job?" I want to suggest strongly that that is only one interpretation and perhaps the least helpful one. "Will it get me a job?" means, of course, will I have something to do when I graduate? It means, help me learn something that will make me feel less frightened, that will help me know that I can cope: Help me picture, prepare for, and face the future. If we take that deep and difficult call to mean only, "Train me for a specific job slot," we will have failed our students.

If, instead, we can step back and ask ourselves yet again what we are doing, and what it does to and for our students, perhaps we can respond more appropriately. I would argue that what we most need to be doing is helping our students learn how to think, and that we haven't the faintest idea how to do that. We are severely hampered in learning how by a tradition designed for only a few among the many we teach today, and even for those few, designed for a past world. The conceptual analysis of what is centrally problematic about the dominant tradition with which it started was discussed so we could analyze what it really might mean to teach thinking, and some thinking about why that matters. In thinking with this conceptual framework in mind, we are in a better position to respond to our own and to our students' need to know why and how what they are studying and what we are teaching matters. We can look at the singular and plural terms, *man* and *men*, *mankind* and *humanity*, and ask just who is in fact intended to be included, and who is intended to be excluded, and why, and with what effects on our thinking. The equity principle of inclusion is not adequate if the newly open room remains suited for only the few. What can't you think about if all that pertains to the maintenance and care of life is considered trivial because it has been relegated for so long to the deprived state of the private realm, the women's sphere? We can make an effort to see singular works and figures and concepts and theories, in context, not as products caused by their condition (not reductively) but as real products of human minds that think always in situations with the tools presently available and according to the prevailing rules of conversation. We can then demystify human achievement, which is never only, and rarely mostly, individual. We can draw connections with and for our students between what they are studying and our shared present world, exploring implications, asking for experiences, unlearning the terrible academic fear of anecdote (which always says to me that *we* don't know how to move from the personal to the intellectual and so blame students for intruding on the material with which we do feel safe).

We can, over and over again, ask with our students, "What does that mean?" and not just, "What does that say?" and then we can ask, "And how do you judge it?" because it is thinking that prepares us to be able to judge, and it is judgment that is required of us if we are to be genuinely independent adults capable of dealing with a demanding, difficult, changing world.

Those are all ways of teaching that apply, and will appeal or not, whether we are speaking as feminists or as regular old dedicated teachers and scholars. But it is my belief that once you have realized that women are not represented in the curriculum as subject matter or as authors and cannot be while *he* is believed to refer to us all, you have opened the door to being able to take on the same questions we have all dealt with adequately, as we could not before. We cannot honestly get to teaching thinking, and developing judgment, if we do not take on the gender exclusivity and its intertwining with race and class bias of our whole tradition. Because if we blithely overlook the fact of the exclusion and/or devaluation of more than half of the human race, how can we possibly be teaching anyone how to read critically, to think things through, to judge? And why should our students believe that we think they matter if we ignore the fact, again, that they sit before us representing two historically, socially, politically, economically, and educationally created "opposite" genders?

So, we can begin to question what we teach to see what it reveals about gender issues. I can guarantee you that your students will be interested—some will be delighted, some will be titillated, some will be infuriated. They will not sit there wondering if it all matters. Then, once that naiveté-shattering issue has been raised, we can begin to add material from the vast body of feminist scholarship now available to help us and our students begin to deal with all subjects with both eyes wide open. The reasons for adding new material, then, are suggested by the following needs: To fill in missing information, once it is recognized that it is, indeed, missing; to raise better, more subtle questions (after all, all women are not, in fact, alike, any more than all men are, in fact, alike *or* are all of humanity); to open up the possibility of dealing with realms of human experience heretofore left blank. That last reason takes us back to curriculum, and why we teach what we do, believing all the while that it may not be career oriented but is nevertheless useful.

Why is it useful? Why is a liberal arts education useful? Originally, it was an entrée for the few privileged males into the ruling positions that would be theirs by birth possibility, if not right. It taught them the language of their culture, its skills and graces and principles and intellectual challenges, as well as the content judged worthy of being known by free men (that is, it was not to be technical or domestic knowledge). Such a model perforce excluded the languages, cultures, skills, and graces and principles and intellectual challenges of and content necessary to the majority of humanity. Women and nonprivileged men were finally allowed to enter the academy; we, today, can finally allow ourselves to feel what they felt, and to claim their pain, unacknowledged as it so often was then, for our own instead of continuing to identify "up." Of course, the outsiders let in were exceptions. As such they lived a discrepancy; they struggled to learn the same things their privileged white male classmates learned but could not possibly have been having the same experience. The irony of being privileged to become simultaneously branded as what you are (a female student; a black student; a scholarship boy) and to deny and to denigrate it at the same time just as almost every work in the curriculum (and most teachers and counselors and day-by-day life) denigrated it, went unrecognized. One was to be grateful. One walked around as W. E. B. DuBois said so eloquently in 1903 with a "double consciousness," "two souls warring in one body," in his language a black man and an American.[4]

A similar experience has been and still is the lot of women. The majority of humanity right now consists of third-world women. How many third-world women are represented on our reading lists, on our faculties, in our administrations, in our dorms, in student offices, in the portraits hanging in our official buildings, on our named scholarship lists? How many times are third-world women, are any women, represented as subject matter in courses, in the campus newspaper ("coed" doesn't count, not when males are the only "students"), in the forums held on campus? If you were a Martian visiting and analyzing your university's curriculum, what kind of human being would you guess was the majority? With such a discrepancy between us and the world, how can we possibly be preparing our students to live honestly? Will they be able to comprehend those with whom they share the world with anything like the intelligence, empathy, and imagination they will need?

And what will they, and we, lose if none of us take on the need to teach the dominant tradition as one among many, as a kind of study rather than as the kind? Start again with those not included, with most of us. What do we lose? We lose the chance to share in the experience of encountering ourselves in works and creations that lift shared, everyday realities onto the plane of thought and imagination, of seeing our-

---

4. W. E. B. DuBois, *Souls of Black Folk* (New York: Signet Classics, New American Library), Chapter 1.

selves as one among many, both the same and different from us yet not other than us. Our feelings are named for us by great thinkers and writers and scholars, by psychologists, philosophers, historians, poets. If they are not named for us, they become, as Arendt put it, our fate. They push and pull us, yet we cannot meet them. Our thoughts, similarly, lead us around, illuminate and confuse us, until or unless we meet someone whose thinking makes sense to us. . . . and I do not mean, by that, whose thinking we can figure out, or follow, or "master." I mean something much more intimate, like the experience of finding a friend. We should all have the chance to find such a thinker in the time we spend in school. I do not believe that at this point the majority of humankind has anywhere near as much chance of having such a soul and sanity-enriching experience as the minority, men, which do. I have to abstract myself a bit to think with men who have already purposefully excluded me from their definition of humanity, after all.

All of us, female and male, also lose the chance to think and feel more fully, with more different voices speaking more widely about the human experience. I recently read a paper by a philosopher who decided to take seriously the notion that human activities, pursued over time as part of accepted cultural roles, are informed by particular modes of thought (as science, for example, can be described as a particular kind of intellectual activity—and as political activity can be, and military strategy, and even the creative process). She looked at motherhood and asked what kind of thinking that experience, sustained as an activity, develops.[5] It is a fascinating article that adds significantly to our notions of humankind and takes us a giant step toward figuring out what it might really mean to say, "Women are more nurturing than men," without being forced back to some kind of biological determinism that is contradicted by almost everything else we teach. Women have been "explained" as products of physiology and of socialization. This new work allows the observation that the "women's work" we have done is also thinking. After all these centuries of thought, we still had no other such analysis of women's thought.

5. Sara Ruddick, "Maternal Thinking," *Feminist Studies* 6:2 (Summer 1980).

But now we do. We can now introduce some fine works of philosophy, of literature, of science, of anthropology, of history to our students that do deal with motherhood, to stay with that example, as experience, as cultural role, as institution, as mode of thought, as myth, as political issue and factor. And we should do so. It's hardly an insignificant subject. We can do the same with materials on rape, and if there is anyone left who does not think that is a critical issue around which questions of serious intellectual, political, personal, cross-cultural significance cluster, I don't know where he or she has been hiding. It is time we made our curriculum sexy. The medieval monks and other men who shaped the "liberal" arts may not have wanted to do so, but what excuse have we? There is superb material, and it is time we became willing to think about it with our students. The only alternative is to hang onto what we were taught as we were taught it as if it were, indeed, the standard of excellence, of disinterestedness, of intellectual rigor and, alone among human products, carried no taint whatsoever, or none worth mentioning, of the prejudices of the few, the partiality of the thinking of the times in which it was created. Do we believe that? If we do, we are also hanging onto the belief that its creators were, indeed, superhuman, and we are their priests, their interpreters to the novitiate. What kind of strength and independence and judgment does that model create?

Hannah Arendt also argued that the modern world is characterized by the loss of authority.[6] I believe that is true, that we already know that the wisdom of the past, however admirable, does not speak to us at the source of our being and cannot command our obedience simply out of respect. Even if we wanted it to, it can't, because the world is too different. To follow them we would have to interpret, and then we would already have begun to exercise the modern need to face a reality for which nothing has prepared us. No, we have to think for ourselves now, and we have to judge. If we begin to think more freely, to take past authorities as voices with whom we can valuably converse but whom we cannot follow, we will have to claim ourselves as people who can judge. And that takes courage. It is deeply tempting to say,

---

6. Hannah Arendt, "Authority," in *Between Past and Future* (New York: Viking, 1968).

"But who am I to judge?" and retreat to passing on the facts or doing exegesis. It even seems the compassionate thing to do, and to say. But if not us, who? And if not now, when?

That brings me back to our expressed desire to help our students, women and men, become strong, independent, resourceful, creative, and successful adults. Can they, as men, attain all those qualities they need if we hand on to them the dominant tradition's view of over half the human race as inferior to them? Such a view requires them to find evidence of their own superiority to the majority of humankind in order simply to be the sex they were born, in order to "be a man." How strong does it make them, to need to live an unexamined lie? How independent? How creative, if all qualities not defined as manly are refused them? Can they, as women, attain all those qualities if they have no past, no stories of their own, no pride in themselves and their mothers and foremothers and all they did and thought? Can they, if their only models of greatness are narrowly defined men? Can they, if each one alone faces the reality of her life as if it were only hers, her fate and not her inheritance? How can they learn to judge, to take that risk, wisely and compassionately and courageously, if they have not learned to think within and about reality, their reality and not that of a singular, universal, white, aristocratic, leisured man?

It is a tribute to the human spirit and mind that many have learned to think and to judge and to act. Had they not, we would not be here today, at a college that has long been dedicated to the education of women, asking all these questions together, and ready to respond to them backed up by a staggering amount of superb new scholarship, and old, retrieved thought and creations once before given to a world not ready to hear. Irony has a way of leaving room for those sensitive to it, and irony we have had. Think what we can do now, with an honesty that prefers the complexity of reality, the clarity of truth, and the enrichment of difference among which none are branded as "other."

We can start asking new questions in class tomorrow. We can start rethinking courses to be sure that over half the human race is not left out. We can establish Women's Studies departments that give a secure base to scholars whose thinking and knowledge about women we all need, who will create the works we need to be more truthful in our own research and teaching. We can work together across disciplines to understand what this new scholarship and those old, silenced voices are saying for all human knowledge, and humane lives. We can examine our own institutions as we would have our students examine their lives, the country they will inherit as citizens, the world in which we all must live so that we and they learn how to understand institutions, and how to act to make them better.

It is, in fact, very easy. That it isn't simply happening is just proof, if we needed any, that the final irony of irony is that it becomes enshrined as the simple, ego-founding, culture-preserving truth. So, to come full circle, perhaps where we start first of all is in recognizing how much energy we are presently wasting trying not to see what is obvious. Unacademic as it may sound, let's start with the obvious, who are we teaching about, how, and for whom? Let me close with a list of ideas that have emerged from feminist scholarship, among them many I have already mentioned today. These notions can be used as organizing principles for classes; as themes for curricula, programs, single courses; as perspectives on what we already include; as suggestions for possible research areas.

- The dominant tradition has emphasized rhetoric, public speech, the creation of a singular character. Conversation, private speech, the creation of interpersonal relationships, have been left out. Rhetoric alone was one of the liberal arts.
- Sameness has been emphasized over difference, leading to the creation of the categories "same" versus "other," where one part of the pair is a negation only. Difference is at least as interesting.
- Sex and gender have been conflated, as if in this one area of human life, nature and culture are to be reduced to nature with barely a residue. If we are to know ourselves, knowing about sex and gender is at least as basic as knowing about men and wars.
- Mortality has been made central to our thought: "Man is mortal" is one of our defining characteristics. Natality has not. And notice we may die alone but we are not born alone—singularity need not be the human condition.
- We have been stuck for centuries with metaphors under-

lying our systems of thought and explanation that are object-centered and make of both change and relation problems: There are now ways of thinking and speaking about context and about process that simply remove those problems.
- The very few who are on top have provided the dominant view of themselves and of us. Our perspective promises to be a great deal more interesting: We haven't the vicious luxury of claiming the world is as we want to define it.
- As we have realized that language varies between subcultures, that systems of meaning are much richer than are reflected in the controlled speech of the few, we have opened up the possibility of studying language itself in new ways.
- Reason, understanding, technical knowledge, logic have all been distinguished among our mental operations. Intuition has not—it is used as the ether or the humours of the blood once were, to name in place of explaining what is obviously going on, as when a woman says something brilliant. Intuition could be studied.
- The few who have written and spoken about equality have simultaneously restricted it to *man*. What happens if we go through those discussions again, with all of us present this time? For one thing, we won't continue to confuse *sameness* with *equality*.
- Research has usually been done about people. What happens when the objects of research used by researchers for their own ends become subjects, help pose the questions and evaluate the results? What happens when research becomes a process of self-discovery and produces knowledge of interest and use?

This list is open-ended—our new curricula are being created now, and by us. They are informed by the question, what will happen when we finally set out to study humankind for the very first time in human history? Can we now make of the inheritance of the past a strengthening study for all of us, rather than an inheritance for the already rich, and a fate for all others?

Alison Bernstein underscores a point during her response to Bernice Sandler in the session focusing on women as agents of change.

Jeanine Elliott

The Curriculum
Summary, Session 3

Who is being taught affects what is being taught. The interaction between the learner and the historic tradition produces what a society believes knowledge to be. Faculties serve as gatekeepers preserving the integrity of the academic tradition and providing a filter between student individualities and the academic discipline. If the historic tradition evolves through the experience and education of men, and if college faculties preserve the integrity of that tradition, then women learners will have only marginal impact upon the college curriculum. Elizabeth Minnich's address presented the limitations of the "partial, singular tradition" in which women have been absent. The respondents, Arthur Levine and Eva Hooker, provided additional perspectives on the connections that exist among the content of the curriculum, the learner, and the transmission of knowledge.

Levine, who is a strong advocate for the liberal arts in education, described the curriculum as a bridge between a college's image of what its graduates should be and the specific students who attend that college. According to Levine, these specific students of today see themselves, as people who believe that the ship they are on is going down and they have a right to have their voyage a luxurious one, that is, to travel "first class." Under these circumstances, financial success becomes the primary consideration in one's education. Knowledge will need to be useful; knowledge will need to lead to a fair income.

The concerns of students are often not the concerns held by college faculties. As society has begun demanding more accountability from the schools, educators emphasize the need for basic skills. In addition to basic skills, Levine affirms a curriculum that includes the knowledge of the way that we live our lives as members of groups and institutions. It should include knowledge of the symbols used to communicate the human heritage, as well as providing a global perspective that reflects the activities common to all human lives. It should include the values that give shape to life. This curriculum could bring a student to the place where she will meet the expectations of her college for its graduates.

Eva Hooker called for a curriculum of "spiritual attention" in her response to the Minnich address. Such a curriculum would teach women to hone their souls as well as their minds. Contemplation as well as analysis would be included in this curriculum. Conference participants were asked to join Hooker in a journey for the search for the "curricular woman," the person in the liberal arts tradition through whom the woman student sees herself. Hooker said that no such woman is to be found, for there are no stories, no myths, no dreams in the curriculum which do not impoverish her.

The curricular story in the traditional disciplines is, according to Hooker, an adventure, a quest. The woman student receives this adventure, as the adventure of the young man, a young man who is in search of "a kingdom, a nation, a chair of governance, a chair of finance, a ladder up and out." The woman exists in it as his dream, his hope, his possibility. "She is not inside a dream about what it means either to be herself or to make herself public." The aims of education belong to his "other-ache," his image of her relationship to him. They do not belong to her.

A college for woman, said Hooker, must "dare to move into the territory of the spirit." Three phases of the journey were presented. The first phase is the power to recognize that which violates the spirit. This must be followed by the power to metamorphose the spirit. In the third phase, the student would gain the capacity to expand the spirit so that she could explain herself both to herself and to others.

Hooker's three stages of spiritual journey parallel Gerda Lerner's stages of feminist consciousness described during the second address to the Symposium. Lerner's analysis is social and historical; Hooker's is spiritual and immediate.

Viewed together, they reflect the connections between social change and personal change. Both progressions will be required of women scholars and students if their experience and knowledge is to be more than marginally represented in the college curriculum.

Woman's lives, viewed historically and in the contemporary setting, will continue to serve as a reminder to the academy that the intellectual assumptions that have undergirded the major academic disciplines are not adequate. The problems of equality and diversity, the value of corporeal existence, the relationship of the body and mind or body and spirit, the needs of the individual over against the needs of the society, the threat of death and the hope of life, the split between thought and action, knowledge and skill, subject and object, the I and the not-I, all of these are intellectual issues addressed in one or more of the academic disciplines. All of these are male intellectual problems; all of these are integrated in women's knowledge and experience. Gerda Lerner captured this concept in her closing comment to this session, "People who take care of daily life—nurturance, death, dirt—never have to worry about practical applications for their knowledge. They live it."

Bernice Resnick Sandler answers questions following her address, "How to Grow 'Movers' and 'Shakers.'"

Bernice Resnick Sandler

Educating Women for Change: How to Grow "Movers" and "Shakers"

One of the latest educational clichés is that we must educate our students to respond to a rapidly changing world. But little has been said about how to teach students to become part of the change process itself—how to become a changer rather than someone who merely responds or adjusts well to change.

When any change occurs, all of us experience some anxiety. Perhaps it is the loss of the familiar, or the fear of the new. Whatever the anxiety is based upon, one of the best ways to mimimize the anxiety of change—or any other anxiety—is to actively participate in the process of that change, i.e., to do something. We can better handle rapid and great changes in our lives and in society if we become part of the process and become actively involved in change itself rather than merely passively responding and adjusting. It's hard to feel helpless when you are actively doing something. When people participate in the process of change, they are less threatened by it.

Definitions of Change

Change, in the broadest terms, is to actively and deliberately behave in such a way so that something becomes different, either in one's own life or in the world at large. If we are uncomfortable about something, whether ourselves, someone else, or something out there in the world, we must first ask, "What can I do about it?" Being a changer means being in control of and responsible for one's self, and making choices based on the potential to change something. To state the obvious, the only way to change one's own life is to behave differently than one has done before. (Perhaps the only way to change someone else's behavior is again to behave *differently* and hope that the other(s) will change in response to the new behavior.)

By changing society, I mean changes in the rules, policies, practices, procedures, laws, and programs that determine the course of events. *Society* can be the informal set of practices of the dormitory or the laws that govern the United States; the policies of a local employer or the organization of international trade.

Eve is perhaps the first woman who can be referred to as "a change agent." She decided to taste the apple, in contrast with Adam, for Eve is a mover and Adam is not.[1] Eve contemplates her decision; she discusses its theological implications with the serpent. She thus is making a considered decision to taste the apple. Adam does not make a considered decision. Eve merely gives him the apple to eat and he does so, without question or comment. Both have eaten of the apple but their behavior is very different; Eve is active and independent; Adam is acquiescent, passive, and unthinking. Eve is truly capable of making change; Adam is merely a follower of others.

If women are to participate fully in the world, they must participate in that world as movers and shakers. Yet something seems to inhibit women from being like Eve. What is it that keeps them from trying to change their lives or the world in which they live? What are the notions that inhibit women from doing this? Let me describe some of the familiar ways in which women and girls learn not to be doers.

Women Learn to Be Passive

Despite many changes in our society concerning the rights of women and changes in their status and roles, most girls and women are still socialized very differently than men. They learn that they are supposed to be more passive than males—an often self-fulfilling prophecy. Too often boys are encouraged to be active while girls are not. For example,

---

1. See Phyllis Trible, "Depatriarchalizing in Biblical Interpretation" in *The Jewish Woman*, edited by Elizabeth Koltan (N.Y.: Schocken Books, 1976).

our response to a boy who is having difficulty coming down from a tree is more likely to be, "Come on, Charlie, you can do it," and to a girl in a similar position, "Hold on, dear, I'll come and get you." If one looks at the pictures and stories in children's books, boys and men are engaged in all kinds of interesting activities, while all too often girls and women are still merely watching and waiting. The message to boys is that it is good for them to take charge of themselves and their lives and to become independent. Girls learn something else—they are encouraged to become dependent upon others.

Thus, women often become vicarious achievers. Instead of becoming the doctor, they marry him. Instead of developing their own talents, they take pride primarily in developing the talents of their husbands and their sons, and occasionally, their daughters. They become the cheerleaders, not the players. It is easier and safer for women to enable and encourage others to develop their abilities. In fact, there is nothing wrong with enabling others; it is a quality that needs to be encouraged in men as well as in women. Too many women, however, enable and empower others at the expense of developing their own talents, abilities, and activities.

Being a "Doer" may be Viewed Being in Conflict with Being "Feminine"

At a deeper level, being a mover and a shaker means being active and effective, which may conflict with one's sense of being a woman. "Real men" don't eat quiche, and "real women" are not movers and shakers. And who would want to be, if they are going to be labeled "castrating," "bitchy," or "one of those women's libbers." How often have we heard women in power described as "The Iron Maiden" or "The Dragon Lady?" The message to both women and men is that achieving women—women who make changes because they are in charge of themselves—are not looked upon favorably.

Old stereotypes about women do not die easily. Even though most women now plan to work for most of their adult lives—whether they marry or not, whether they take time off for raising children—most of them still carry outdated notions of what constitutes femininity. Women learn to be pleasant and to smile—some of us cannot even talk about the most serious of subjects without smiling. We learn to be modest and often find it easier to talk about our failures (sometimes humorously) than about our achievements.

Society gives women very mixed expectations. On the one hand we are told that all the opportunities are ours, and on the other hand we are subtly reminded that to have power, i.e., to be effective and able to cause change, may be a mixed blessing and that it is not the same as it is for men. It is hard enough to go against society's stereotypes but it is even more frightening to face the possible loss of close relationships. Success, power, and effectiveness make men sexy; the same characteristics in a woman will make some men (not all, fortunately) most uncomfortable. Many young men, while stating their belief in equal rights for women, are still not so sure that they want to marry women with strong careers—careers that might be as important as theirs.

Moreover, power, and strength for women—a definition of the ability to make change—are often erroneously viewed or confused by women as being synonomous with being selfish, manipulative, and/or destructive.[2] For too many women, especially, to act in one's own interest and for one's own motivation may not be experienced as satisfying or exhilarating but perceived as a frightening thing to do. Jean Baker Miller notes that for some women, acting in their own interest as a mature person, is experienced as "the psychic equivalent of being a destructively aggressive person . . . a self image which few women can bear."[3] It is better to feel helpless, dependent, and inadequate than to feel destructive. All of these stereotypes and expectations have a cumulative effect. Without a woman's even knowing it, she is subtly discouraged in a thousand ways from becoming a mover and a shaker.

Lack of Role Models

Even if women struggle against or do not accept those notions, even if they are ready to take on leadership roles and change, they still cannot easily become movers and shakers for other reasons. They lack role models which portray women as movers. Who shall they model themselves

---

2. See, for example, Jean Baker Miller, "Colloquium: Women and Power," Work in Progress No. 82-01, Stone Center for Developmental Services and Studies, Wellesley College, Wellesley, MA.

3. Ibid., p. 4.

after? Lady Macbeth? Betsy Ross? Miss Piggy? Where are the women administrators in the school they attend? Where are women in television, movies, theater, and books who are active, fully functioning human beings, and who also have a husband and children?

Lack of Confidence

Yet another factor is lack of confidence. For a variety of reasons (too numerous to detail here) many women have little confidence in their abilities. Indeed, numerous studies have shown that when a male is successful at a task, it is typically attributed to his talents, skills, and hard work; for a female, in contrast, her achievements are more likely to be attributed to luck and happenstance, or to attributes beyond her control, such as an easy assignment, or the fact that her boss liked her. Thus women may have little awareness of their abilities and take little pride in what they do. Compliment a woman's activities, clothes, or accomplishments, and you are far more likely to get explanations such as: "It's just an *old* dress I made," or "Anyone could have done it," or most likely in the case of considerable achievement, "I was very lucky." These reactions indicate that many women considerably underestimate their abilities and potential and lack the confidence that is necessary in order to take risks, to be a mover, and to be perceived as a person capable of being able to effect change.

Limited Knowledge and/or Experience with Being a Changer

If all of this were not enough to actively or subtly discourage women from becoming the kind of people who make changes in this world, women face at least two more obstacles. One, they may have little knowledge of how to make changes happen and, two, just as important, having been cast in the role of conserver and passive onlooker, they may have little experience in actually making things change.

What Can a College Do to Help Women Become Movers and Shakers?

We come back now to the subject of this paper: How can a college help its women students become effective movers and shakers? Although my comments are directed at all colleges, I want to focus first on women's colleges.

The College as a Counterbalance to Society

If a women's college is to have any justification, it must provide a setting and a framework in which women can flourish and develop in ways that they cannot readily do so at other institutions and elsewhere in the society. If a women's college is to be truly useful to the women who attend it, it must deliberately act as a counterbalance to trends and stereotypes in our society that hinder and hurt the development of women into all they have the potential for.

The women's college must deliberately set out to provide a different kind of experience from what women would find elsewhere. It must provide a singular atmosphere where women examine and evaluate their lives as women, where students and faculty together deliberately and consciously set out to explore what it means to be a woman in our society. It must be a place where patterns of discrimination—overt and subtle—are discussed and analyzed. It must be a place that consciously sets out to weaken the effects of the negative stereotypes to which their students have been exposed from very early in life. It must help women examine those stereotpyes, behaviors, rules, laws and other constraints that affect their lives as women. Of course we must do this in coeducational as well as in single-sex institutions. How do we do this?

The Curriculum

The curriculum is one of the strongest tools that a college has to affect the lives of its students, to help them understand their role as women in society, to give them the confidence they need in order to effect change, and to free them from the constraints that society has placed upon them. The curriculum gives students very powerful messages, although not always overtly articulated or acknowledged. We can begin to counteract the notion of female as passive through the content in a variety of disciplines.

History provides us with many examples. Women's role in

ancient and modern history has been largely overlooked, and hence the need to re-examine history in our plan to educate women for change. For instance, most of us were taught very little about how women obtained the right to vote in the United States. In all likelihood most of us learned that women were *given* the vote in 1920. Given by whom? The implication is that men gave women the vote and that women were passive and had little to do with it. In fact, women throughout the United States actively struggled for suffrage from 1868 to 1920. In order to obtain the right to vote, women conducted

480 campaigns to get state legislatures to submit suffrage amendments to voters;

56 campaigns of referendums to voters;

47 campaigns to get state constitutional conventions to write women's suffrage into state constitutions;

277 campaigns to get state party conventions to include women's suffrage planks;

30 campaigns to get presidential party conventions to do the same; and

19 campaigns with 19 successive Congresses.[4]

And this doesn't include the ratification campaigns in the states after Congress passed the Nineteenth Amendment. To study the history of the suffrage gives us a very different picture of women than the one conjured up by the words, "The vote was given to women." We need to know more about our role in history and about the magnificent women who belie the notion of women as passive; history can provide us with sorely needed role models. History can also provide women (and men) with the belief that women can indeed play a role in changing society.

The notion of passivity could also be examined in a variety of courses. Psychology and sociology classes could examine how families and society encourage or discourage boys and girls from being passive. What happens to males and females who don't conform to sexual stereotypes? How does the concept of women-as-passive affect how they are treated in law, in the workplace, in school and elsewhere? Anthro-

4. Carrie Chapman Catt and Nettie Rogers Shuler, *Woman Suffrage and Politics* (N.Y.: Scribners, 1923), p. 107.

pology classes could explore whether "passivity" of women exists in other cultures. Biology could explore whether the "passivity" of females occurs in other species, e.g., female lions are usually the hunters, not the males. Education classes could examine textbooks and their portrayal of females as contrasted to males. Literature courses could examine the great novels in the same way, as could art history examine the great works of the world.

All of these "lessons"—already being taught in many classrooms—would help young women and men understand more about themselves and the world they live in. They would get a very different message about the "passivity" of women.

Throughout the curriculum, we must ask what difference a person's sex makes in all social, political, cultural, and economic life. Because the new scholarship on women asks different questions, it is very much like having new glasses. Old knowledge suddenly looks different. New connections are made, and knowledge is being given new shape as the curriculum begins to encompass all of the human race.

Let me come back to Eve again and show you how, by looking at the story with different glasses, we see a very different Eve than the one we have been taught about, an Eve who now gives us a very different message. Phyllis Trible deserves credit for this analysis.

> the woman [Eve] is more appealing than her husband. Throughout the myth she is the more intelligent one, the more aggressive one and the one with greater sensibilities. . . . The initiative and the decision are hers alone. She seeks neither her husband's advice nor his permission. She acts independently. By contrast, the man is a silent and bland recipient. "She also gave some to her husband and he ate." . . . His one act is belly-oriented, and it is an act of quiescense, not of initiative. The man is not dominant; he is not aggressive; he is not a decision-maker. . . . He follows his wife without . . . comment, thereby denying his own individuality. If the woman be intelligent, sensitive and ingenious, the man is passive, brutish and inept.[5]

We are not only talking about subject matter about women in a particular course in religion or elsewhere, or a separate

---

5. Trible, "Depatriarchalizing in Biblical Interpretation."

course about women. We need to do more than just "add women to the curriculum and stir."[6] We are talking about a total transformation of the entire curriculum. While it is inappropriate here to discuss women's studies in detail, I do want to point out that the new scholarship on women is already enriching the curriculum and our perspectives in the various disciplines. The new curriculum is one of the strongest means we have to help women develop into movers and shakers.

When women begin to examine their lives *as women in our society*—when they see how discrimination against women has affected them; when they confront their own experiences as women; when they can understand how women are treated differently in a host of subtle ways—only then it is possible for them to build new sources of strength within themselves and to cast off old stereotypes that constrain their lives. Without this, there cannot be the confidence in one's self that is essential to being able to be an effective mover or shaker.

It is in this area—re-examining the role of women—that women's studies can be of enormous help. Anyone who has looked at the extensive reading lists of many of these courses knows that they are not frivolous but highly academic. For many women, these courses serve a very real purpose in helping them to examine themselves as women for the *first* time in their lives; they can create a revolution in female identity. By confronting themselves as women, they can begin to deal with the contradictions and conflicts in their lives. For this purpose, studying about women, whether in separate courses, programs or in a transformed curriculum, serves a unique role, for unlike other academic content, they are *directly* relevant to the lives of students. They are consciousness raising with intelligence and without hysteria. They are useful to men as well as women in providing them with greater understanding of the lives of women. Innumerable students report that these courses have literally changed their lives. They feel freer, more active, more willing to make changes, more confident about their abilities. In short, they are on the way to becoming movers and shakers.

6. The writer is grateful to Margaret McIntosh of the Wellesley College Center for Research on Women for this notion.

Classroom behavior

What happens in the classroom apart from curriculum can also affect women in other ways as well. Although most teachers want to be fair to their students, men and women faculty alike often treat men and women students very differently. The behavior is typically invisible—neither students nor faculty are aware that any differential behavior has occurred. The Project on the Status and the Education of Women recently published a report on this subject and identified more than thirty types of behaviors in which women students may be treated differently.[7] Women students, for example, are more likely to be interrupted and are called upon less. Faculty are more apt to look directly at men students when they ask a question of the class, thereby communicating that they expect the men to answer. Men's names are more likely to be remembered than those of the women. These behaviors, when taken singly, may well seem trivial, but when taken together they form an insidious pattern that has a devastating effect upon the confidence of women students. Their participation in class is subtly discouraged by these behaviors, and passivity encouraged. These behaviors, alas, are not limited to the classroom but occur in many of the ordinary everyday interchanges between women and men. If women are to function fully, the college must help them to become aware of these subtle behaviors so that they are not harmed by them. The college must also help faculty learn to recognize these differential behaviors so they will indeed treat their students more fairly. Our report identified more than one hundred ways in which institutions can do this.

Using the Curriculum to Study Change

We will also need to use the curriculum to explore various concepts of change so that women understand the process of bringing about change. In order to underscore the importance of change and how it occurs, an institution would

---

7. See *The Classroom Climate: A Chilly One for Women?*, Roberta M. Hall with the assistance of Bernice R. Sandler, Project on the Status and Education of Women, Association of American Colleges, 1818 R Street, N.W., Washington, D.C. 20009. $3.00 prepaid.

need to explicitly devote time and resources to the examination of concepts about change itself. This could be done through seminars, conferences, or perhaps there could be a day or week (or more) when a large number of classes throughout the campus could discuss these issues. Change could be the theme for an intersession curriculum, or for an honors project, or for a specific interdisciplinary program. For example, to use history again, the focus could be not only on particular changes but why and how a particular change occurred. Who were the players and how did they do it? Who were the movers and shakers? What role did women play and if none, why? What happens to women "movers"? What happened to Eve? Does that happen to women today? What are the risks of being a changer? Similar questions could be addressed in political science classes. Sociology could examine how change occurs and how groups respond; and psychology classes could do the same in examining how individuals change and why change may be difficult for some women. Philosophical aspects of change could be addressed, as well as biological notions about physical changes. What is really called for is an interdisciplinary focus on exploring concepts of change by having virtually the entire curriculum address these issues and an exploration of how each discipline can contribute to our understanding of the change process.

Beyond the formal curriculum, students will need experience in observing and analyzing change as well as gaining experience in situations where change is occurring. For example, internships whether in an advocacy organization or in a business or nonprofit setting can help sharpen students' understanding of change. They can seek answers from their experience to questions such as the following: What changes occurred? What changes were resisted? Who were the important players? Who had the power to make the changes? What pressure were they vulnerable to? Who was in a position to get these pressures exerted? Who were the resisters? What tactics and strategies were used—which worked and which did not? How was timing important?

Students can obtain even more specific experience regarding change by assigning each student a "change project." Students can be asked to select something that they want to change. It might be as small as changing an informal classroom or domitory practice; it might be as large as changing a federal regulation. Students could act separately or work with others. They could join an organization already engaged on their chosen issue or they can do any of a variety of activities to help them analyze the factors that are needed in order to accomplish the change. The success of their project would not necessarily be judged on their achieving the change but on the student's analysis of the process, including answers to questions about change raised above, similar to those mentioned earlier.

But even all this would not be enough. Special efforts will also need to be made in order to develop women's sense of self and confidence.

Increasing Women's Confidence Through Sports Participation

One way to increase women's confidence is through athletics. Physical activity, whether jogging or gymnastics, hockey or hiking, can have a profound impact on self-confidence. In team sports, one also learns how to respond to loss without a debilitating sense of failure—there is always another game in which to test oneself. Sports also teach teamwork and how to develop new strategies. Sports develop leadership in part because they allow the participants to test themselves without a loss of self.

Will Women Be More Humane When They Become Changers?

The basic question concerns whether women can shape the future in more humane ways if they are prepared to participate in and guide the change process. I believe that the answer is yes. Although women have been socialized in many ways that denigrate them and restrict their abilities, at the same time they have also generally learned to behave in a more civilized manner than their brothers. Carol Gilligan notes that men's concepts of justice are generally based on notions of individual rights; women's concepts are generally based on notions of responsibility for others.[8] For centuries

---

8. Carol Gilligan, *In a Different Voice*.

human beings have struggled with ways to end wars and violence, often concluding that this was just "human nature." Perhaps if we look at how women are socialized for nonviolence, we might indeed learn some lessons about how to curb the violence of mankind.

But it would also be foolish to believe that all women are going to be more humane than all men. There have always been men and women who have gone beyond the stereotypes of their sex. As the socialization of women changes, however, there is a danger that some women may become less caring and less humane as their focus shifts to more personal fulfillment. Colleges can take deliberate steps to counteract this trend by becoming more humane themselves. They need to be a model of humaneness in their relationships to faculty, staff, and students.

For example, the women's college, as well as others, must increasingly be concerned with the problems of all women, and not just those of the traditional college student. It must reach out actively to older women who want to return to the campus, to poor women who want and need education, to black women and other minority women who need a special helping hand. One of the most fascinating aspects of the women's movement that has hardly been commented on is that it cuts across racial, economic, class, and age lines. It is indeed a most humane movement. Conservative older women work together with young radical college students on issues concerning women, with both profiting from the experience. The women's college can play a major role in encouraging humane values by helping to bridge the gap between different groups of women. It must deliberately and publicly reorganize itself so that its concern is truly that of all women. Part-time studies need to be encouraged, so women with family responsibilities can still complete their education. Evening courses, Saturday courses, short-term courses and off-campus courses need to be explored. Scholarships for part-time students need to be developed for these women. Students who have dropped out because of marriage or whatever reasons should find the door open if they wish to return. Certainly, the transfer of credits and the development of a degree in absentia would ease the burden of those students who have moved and cannot easily return to complete their degree. Residency requirements need to be revamped, again so that women are not penalized but are encouraged to return to school. Dormitory arrangements for married women with children need to be worked out. Child-care services need to be developed so that mothers can continue their education. All of these changes would indicate to students that their institution is not only capable of change, but also that their institution is a caring place and that caring and nurturing are important values.

What is indeed needed in both women's colleges and coeducational institutions is a thorough re-evaluation of all policies and practices and how these policies and practices affect women. By reaching out into the community toward all women, and by making it easier for all women to attend college, the student body will change, for it will include a mixture of women at all ages with differing economic backgrounds and interests. Such a mixture can only be beneficial to all involved. Young women, instead of being isolated for four years with other young women very much like themselves will have more opportunities to understand the varied lives of women and to more realistically evaluate their own future plans. Just as important, they will see women struggling to make changes in their own lives, women who can be important role models.

Leadership Among Students

One of the often extolled virtues of a women's college is the opportunity for leadership. When young men and young women work together on extracurricular projects, they typically follow the pattern that is "normal" for our society: the men play the role of leader, and the women become the secretaries, note takers, and the coffee makers. Many women, if they have only functioned in groups that include men, have rarely had the opportunity to learn or exert leadership. Yet these same young men, if working together without men, will be leaders as well as note takers.

Nevertheless, the women's college, like other colleges, must make a special effort to increase leadership opportunities for its students. To do this, it must treat its students as responsible, active adults. We are all likely to respond in terms of the expectations people have of us. If we treat our women students as passive and unable to make decisions concerning their own lives, then they may indeed act this way. Giving students a greater voice in the running of campus affairs is particularly important if we are to help counteract the notions that women are passive and need to be dominated by others. Women students need to be encouraged to play a large role in decisionmaking on their campuses. We need to treat women the way we want them to behave. Still another, often overlooked, way to develop leadership is the use of assertiveness training.

Providing Role Models

All colleges need to serve another critical function by providing role models of women actively engaged in the world of work, particularly in academic life. It is urgent that young women see older women in a variety of roles and activities that counter the stereotypes in our society. If young women never see a woman scientist, they are likely to continue to believe that women are not, or cannot be, scientists. Young women need to see adult women working so that they can have some sense of the kinds of changes they can make in their own lives. Some of these women will be unmarried, some will be married without children, some will have young children, some will have older children. But all will show the young woman that a variety of life patterns are possible. Women must be visible on the faculty and invited to campus to participate in programs, conferences, receive awards, serve as trustees and as administrators.

Women's institutions as well as coeducational ones should be model employers for women. Our women's colleges especially should surely lead the way in developing similar new policies that enhance the employment of women. Enlightened policies that increase the number of women on the faculty would also serve to increase the number and variety of role models for students; they would lead the way for other institutions to follow, and they would stand as symbolic of the college's commitment to women as faculty, staff, and students.

Female faculty are critical if young women are to change their own perception of themselves. A recent study by M. Elizabeth Tidball found that women listed in *Who's Who of American Women* were more than twice as likely to be graduates of women's colleges than graduates of coeducational institutions. Moreover, the percentage of women "achievers" was directly related to the number of women faculty. She concluded that "As society's need for talent increases, a direct means to develop talent among young women would be to increase the presence and improve the status of women academic professionals. There cannot be one without the other."[9] Moreover, having women on the faculty is not enough; they must be in key administrative positions as well.

Traditionally, and fortunately, women's colleges have had a high proportion of women on their faculties. In fact, the only "coeducational" faculties have generally been at women's colleges. Nevertheless, women's institutions need to do more and become the most hospitable places in the nation for women to work.

To insure the development of leadership, the women's college must provide a uniquely female environment, with women in positions of power, including the presidency. This is not to say that men should not work in these institutions but that the majority of the key administrative posts in a women's college ought to be held by women.

If the women's college is to survive and if it is to truly educate women to become changers, it must do more than merely parrot what is going on elsewhere. It needs to provide a supportive atmosphere where women can unlearn the traditional notions about what a woman's life is like. In this sense, the women's college can help bridge the gap for women caught between these crippling traditional notions and the promise of equality.

True educational equality will come only when we eliminate the stereotypes that limit women and their ambitions. For truly, women are disadvantaged long before they come to college. It should be the clear purpose of all colleges to counteract those disadvantages. In summary, the unique program that a women's college can offer is that of a female environment which deliberately sets out to create a climate that helps women discover and examine their role as women

9. M. Elizabeth Tidball, "Perspective on Academic Women and Affirmative Action," *The Educational Record* (Spring 1973).

in society—a campus that is responsive to all women, and brings together on the campus women of varying ages, varying races, and varying backgrounds; a campus that acknowledges that women are often treated unfairly and differently in our society; a campus that actively seeks to provide a climate in which women can grow to be full human beings. But this mission cannot be limited to women's colleges; our coeducational institutions must have the same concern and commitment if they are to be truly responsive to all their students.

The chance for change is now in the hands of the women's college. No single coeducational institution has shown any major concern for the education of women as an entity. In contrast, many women's colleges, like Stephens, have long examined and question what the education of women is all about. By developing new programs for women faculty and students, by creating a new atmosphere, the women's college can indeed do more than merely survive; it can lead the way for the educational community in developing new ways of working with students which are truly relevant to their lives. And they can become models for the coeducational institutions to follow.

Women have been initiating change since the dawn of history. I began this paper by talking about Eve; let me end it by noting that archeologists and anthropologists now believe that it was women who invented pottery and women who discovered agriculture. That latter discovery led to one of the greatest changes in human history. Nomadic hunters could now settle down long enough to invent written language and the beginnings of complex civilization. Can you imagine what must have happened when one woman or several realized that the seeds discarded during food preparation were responsible for the new plants growing above them. Do you think that the insight that plants could actually be planted was well received? While it is possible that the clan leader said, "What a wonderful discovery!" it is more likely that it was opposed. It must have seemed unnatural, strange and even frightening. Perhaps it was seen as the work of a witch; perhaps the gods would be angry; perhaps the food would be poisoned. Perhaps the women worked together to present their ideas. Whatever the scenario, the women movers and shakers must have persisted and somehow finally convinced the powers that were that this was a useful change.

We have been making changes for a long time, sometimes unnoticed, and without getting credit, and sometimes against great odds. As women's opportunities expand, so will the opportunities for change increase.

Women are a new advocacy group not only on campus, but in the nation as well. Let me close with a quotation that is said to have been found on a tablet discovered by an all-woman team of archeologists, assisted by women staff, and women students:

> And they shall beat their pots and pans into printing presses
> And weave their cloth into protest banners.
> Nations of women shall lift up their voices with nations of other women.
> Neither shall they accept discrimination anymore.[10]

That statement may seem apocryphal, but I suspect it may yet prove to come from the Book of Prophets. For what women are learning is the politics of change. The campus, the nation, the world will never again be the same.

10. From a poster by Mary Chagnon.

Kathy H. Reese

Women as Agents for Change
Summary, Session 4

Cynthia Secor introduced this session as one dealing with woman's need for "free space" in which to develop, change, and hold a true sense of power. She noted that all the presenters are women who have created public space for us all in political, educational, and economical areas of our society.

Bernice Sandler's major theme dealt with how the world needs courageous women, "movers and shakers," who are willing to take control rather than merely responding to a rapidly changing world. Quickly reviewing women's socialization experiences that encourage opposite sorts of behaviors, Sandler concluded that for a women's college to be truly useful, it must consciously choose to act as a counterbalance to the trends and stereotypes that hurt women's development. Women's colleges must create an environment reflecting a "politics of change."

Reactor panelist Alison Bernstein agreed that women must be "movers and shakers," but strongly suggested they must also be guardians of their own structures, values, and behaviors. If women don't do this, she added, then it's sure that men will not. Bernstein suggested four concrete strategies for educating students for social change. Educational institutions must intentionally design a curriculum that will (a) compel students to engage in meaningful social action for others (through off-campus service internships), (b) educate women for nontraditional fields thus infusing feminist consciousness into the nonacademic mainstream, (c) instruct students in the use of technological tools that give them access to an informational society, and (d) teach them

The entire symposium was designed to encourage interchange between speakers, panelists, and participants. Here Kathy Reese of Stephens' Counseling Service poses a question.

to write so we will have a permanent record of our changes for the generations who follow, thereby acting as guardians of our own history.

Gloria Randle Scott, the second respondent on the panel, reminded us that change takes place over generations. Colleges need to ally with elementary schools to make sure social changes for women occur. Scott offered several suggestions for how to produce women who have options and who understand the impact of change. Colleges, she urged, need to challenge women toward immediate, productive involvement in working toward change. Colleges need to show a true racial inclusiveness in their faculties and student body, and challenge uneasiness in dealing with "critical masses" of people who are different from the dominant society. Opportunities to experience many varieties of female role models must be given to students, and radical interventions to produce an egalitarian environment for all segments of educational institutions—students, faculty, administrators, trustees—are crucial. Technological literacy, knowing the code words and phrases of an informational society, must be taught to help give women access to power. We must gain access to funding sources so that research attention will be directed to women's issues. Faculty and student development personnel need to join forces to help to create an informal atmosphere teaching political change. Lastly, colleges must constantly challenge faulty logic that bars women from education or training for full participation in society.

In the discussion that followed, audience attention quickly turned to specific tools women need to create public space or to become politically powerful forces. Bernstein's challenge to "infuse the feminist consciousness into nontraditional fields" was amplified in a lively discussion concerning the importance of teaching math, science, and computer technology to women. Opportunities in these areas need to begin as early as elementary school. Already there are reports of boys seeking out computers in greater numbers than girls and high school girls choosing not to elect computer courses because it make them feel "different or eccentric."

Bernstein pointed out that some institutions such as Alverna College are exploring competency-based education for women, thus ensuring minimum standards for ability in these fields. Bernstein advocated teaching the true political necessity of mastering concepts in science, math, and computer technology, that is, their relation to the control, distribution, and negotiation of social change in an informational society.

Offering opportunities in nontraditional fields, however, does not address the lack of motivation in women to participate in these disciplines. There was broad agreement that deliberate planning is necessary to overcome internalized barriers to achieve in these fields, and several examples of math or computer workshops and programs were discussed. The discussion is probably best summarized by a comment indicating an urgent need to follow up quickly on such suggestions because if women don't, white males will understand and control computers in this age of information.

Sandler pointed out that faculty members often have anxiety about computers. Because this goes unacknowledged, faculty attitudes can become invisible barriers. Discussion led to broader issues and anxieties involving faculty. For example, some faculty are willing to work with women's studies in a narrow academic sense but consider questions of social change inappropriate academically. Participants pondered how to develop strategies for changes in faculty attitudes. It was suggested that faculty must be helped to understand that social change is present in all history, and that we need faculty leaders who are sensitive to the relation of the world and the educational curriculum. Social action itself might be relabeled as good citizenship. Faculty must ask themselves how good citizenship relates to their discipline, especially in the area of women's issues.

Faculty overload and fatigue were argued as reasons for some reluctance to become involved in new areas. One participant noted there is often a "holy trinity" of simultaneous service, teaching, and scholarship expected for faculty performance. An attempt to separate these simultaneous demands is being made at the State University of New York at Stonybrook where faculty may choose to rotate through intense time periods of either service, or scholarship, sequentially. This approach has offered a healthy and revitalizing alternative to the faculty, freeing them for periods of truly intense exploration and involvement.

As the session concluded, the discussion of nontraditional education for women shifted more explicitly to its implications for power in the political arena.[1] There was enthusiastic agreement about the need to educate women to an awareness of political interactional skills such as collaboration and coalition building. Discussants concluded that students need to learn coalition building, collaboration, and conflict management. Women in particular need to learn collegiality in conjunction with the debating of decisions, expressing polar opinions yet remaining collegial toward the person who is opposite. Sandler pointed out that coalition skills are crucial for change. She referred to her involvement in the National Coalition for Women and Girls in Education, a group monitoring what the federal government is doing in relation to women. She emphasized that a coalition gives the appearance and actuality of power. Power is needed to make change. It is the responsibility of educational institutions to help each woman to locate the source of her own power, to approach it proudly, and to share it with other women in the changing of our society.

1. A resource guide is available describing educational programming for women about policies and public leadership. Write to:

Public Leadership Education Network
c/o The Center for the American Woman and Politics
Eagleton Institute of Politics
Rutgers University
New Brunswick, N.J.
Phone (210) 828-2210

William Chafe describes expectations of today's college students.

Bobbie Burk

Synthesis Session

The sixth and final session of the Stephens Symposium was devoted to a synthesis of the conference based on the perceptions of four distinguished participants. The session was moderated by Sheila Tobias who was assisted by Judith Touchton, Carolyn Dorsey, and Cynthia Secor, moderators of earlier sessions. Each raised additional questions that deserve consideration. Tobias reminded us that the traditional liberal arts curriculum has proven to have some measure of effectiveness for women, because it has brought us to the point where we can look critically at education, and it has taught that mastery of knowledge and skills are necessary for the development of leadership potential. Even as the biased content of the traditional curriculum impels us to recognize its limitations, we also have to acknowledge the liberating effects that such study has had in our lives. As the integration of new scholarship begins to transform the traditional curriculum, we are reminded that transmutation has always been an essential part of the pursuit of truth and knowledge and that the pursuit never ends. Scholars and others who work to bring about transition are risk takers, but change will not take place unless risks are taken. Students, women particularly, must be urged not to settle for what has been, but urged instead to stretch, to reach for what should be. At the same time, Tobias said, if change is to be accepted, it will be necessary to tolerate differing levels of feminist philosophy. Otherwise, some might be driven away who would ultimately benefit the most, those who may not believe themselves to be feminists.

Touchton spoke about the importance of "creating visions of the future" through discovering and reclaiming (women's) history. The images thus produced will "drive the conscious mind," providing the motivation needed to continue striving for change. The women's movement has come of age, built upon a long history of the accomplishments of many who worked to re-vision the future. The collective effect of the historical record demonstrates that when women have the time and space to work, profound change takes place. Leadership, however, is crucial. There is a critical lack of women, particularly minority women, in top leadership positions in academic, as well as other, institutions. Awareness of this problem should increase our determination to work toward the placement of women in positions of influence. Projects such as the National Identification Program, sponsored by the American Council on Education, and those sponsored by other professional associations, are designed to build communication networks that further the advancement of talented women in administrative positions. Although not highly visible, women with leadership qualities clearly exist; their potential impact on higher education must not be underestimated. The future is in us; we are the future.

Using a model that examines "access, distribution, and persistence," Dorsey addressed the lack of opportunity for women and minorities to advance in higher education. Although opportunities have increased, the principle problem is still lack of access, heightened by the enrollment distribution of women and minorities whose college careers often begin and end in community colleges. Better articulation agreements should be established between two- and four-year institutions so that more women and minorities are encouraged to continue college work beyond the associate degree level. When these students do transfer to four-year institutions, support systems should be available to help them remain in school long enough to earn baccalaureate degrees. Most women who attend community college are older, part-time students who may need special dispensations when meeting certain degree requirements, such as residency. They are also likely to need child-care assistance. Most women continue to enroll in degree programs that have been traditional fields for females. Women must be helped to develop the self-confidence that allows them to consider alternative careers and then they should be urged to persist, to overcome the barriers and problems that arise to impede their progress, as they work toward their educational and life goals.

Secor drew attention to the difference between women's studies and women's education, and suggested that women's education should be keyed to helping women become autonomous. Since faculty and administrators maintain institutions through the conscious selection of information, it is critical that the information transmitted to women students signal that the institution is truly committed to women's education. When signals are inconsistent, ambivalence rather than autonomy will be fostered. Autonomy assumes "that we are acting out of self, centered (not self-centered) and rooted." Many women need to be resocialized to realize that they have the right to autonomy. Moreover, the achievement of autonomy need not preclude nurturance, an equally important companion in women's education. Nurturance is not limited to interaction between humans, rather, it encompasses all living creatures and natural resources. Can we do anything about the problems caused by aggression? Is it taught, genetically linked, or socialized? What would happen if we refused to teach about war?

Tobias, in closing the formal part of the session, commented on the remarkable consistency of the level of excellence in the presentations made during the symposium. There was a suggestion to establish a summer institute, where speakers could discuss the issues raised by the symposium.

When the session was opened for discussion from the audience, participants contributed observations and comments and continued to raise questions developed out of the themes that ran throughout the conference. We were reminded that students grow through the experiences made available to them, and that although students were present at the symposium in relatively large numbers, and some assumed responsible roles throughout the planning and implementation of the meeting, there had been no student speaker. The value of including a student's viewpoint on issues that are critical in their lives, now and in the future, should not be overlooked. Today's student is the leader of tomorrow. If we hope to have a different type of leader, we must assume the responsibility for opening up opportunities for young women that allow them to practice a different style of leadership, a style that recognizes that the tension between leadership and autonomy can be creative. A feminist leadership style includes accountability, coalition building, and collaborative management, all of which can strengthen individual autonomy while building for collective action. Leaders define; because women see things differently, when they come into leadership roles in greater numbers, the nature of leadership will change.

Among those who work to improve opportunities for women, there is still a tendency, considered by some to be dangerous, to see men constantly as opponents. The danger lies in the assumption that women can bring about change without the involvement of men. The assumption is, in part, defensive action on the part of women and due to the problems females have faced as a result of various developmental theories in which the male model has been promulgated as the norm, thereby indicating superiority and at the same time relegating females to inferior or aberrant status. The work of Carol Gilligan, among others, is questioning such theories. In Gilligan's work, men and women are shown to be much the same (self-centered) at the start, but beyond that point men begin to find their identity through separation, while women find their identity through nurturance. Gilligan's research recognizes that value of plurality and diversity, rather than promoting the polarity of superiority-inferiority. If better balance in society is a goal of women's education, men, too, must be educated for change.

Questions were raised about the influence of research. Has gender-based research been avoided because the results might not be what we want to hear? Should coalitions be developed between small institutions primarily devoted to teaching and larger institutions that sponsor research, in order to promote the practical application of the results of research projects that will advance the influence of women's education? Are political pressures such, on research campuses, that research which focuses on issues related to women and minorities is prevented from taking place? Will the models of research considered acceptable on large campuses allow other, less traditional, models to be seen as valid research? The point was made that research which will make a difference does not have to be done at a larger institution; the work of symposium speakers demonstrates this fact. Smaller liberal arts colleges can not only provide a more hospitable climate for newer forms of research, they can provide the necessary support for faculty research projects through carefully planned released time. With time and space, faculty can do the kind of questioning and inquiry necessary to produce significant results. It is sobering to realize, however, that until women are educated as if they are as capable as men, it will be difficult, if not impossible, to determine whether or not there are real, inherent differences, other than physiological, between males and females.

Linda Orlansky, Helen Astin (respondent), Bobbie Burk, and Nancy Walker discuss the program for the symposium.

Bobbie Burk

Afterword

Even as the symposium proper ends, its proper work begins. Participants left with a renewed vision of what women's education is and what it can accomplish; a vision that transcended the specific issues that shaped the conference:
- The impact of societal change on the lives of women.
- The educational needs of women of varying ages and backgrounds.
- The role of the college curriculum in preparing women for the challenges of the future.
- The preparation of women to become agents of change in society.

Just as the new scholarship on women seeks to transform the curriculum for all who teach and study it, so women's education is a means of transforming educational experiences for students and faculty, males as well as females. The framework that provided the structure for the symposium also established a model for women's education, one that will be a force for change.

The symposium was held, in part, to celebrate the 150th anniversary of Stephens College. The life of the college runs parallel to the history of opportunities for education at the post-secondary level for females in the United States, and the development of the college's programs has reflected the evolutionary nature of thought regarding the purposes of educating women. Much has been accomplished at Stephens College and at other colleges; however, most of the change has taken place in isolated pockets, such as Women's Studies programs, or enclaves, such as women's colleges. Nowhere has change been as pervasive as it should be. This knowledge keeps us from being deluded about the scope of accomplishment and from becoming complacent about it; there is much yet to be done. Change is slow, it is difficult, and it is often painful; but with administrative and financial support it can be brought about. The model articulated by the symposium will apply toward that end.

Perhaps the single greatest task ahead is the integration of the new scholarship on women into the curriculum. The enormity of the integration task stuns the academic mind, conscious of the time and energy required to revise one course or to change degree requirements. We can, however, take heart in the example of gradual acceptance received by Women's Studies programs and in the successes of various college and university integration projects which also serve as models for change. It will take individual and concerted effort to offset the problems caused by centuries of misinformation and incomplete information. Many faculty will be threatened by the revolutionary nature of the scholarly, philosophical, and pedagogical impact that women's education has on the academy; those who give the issues fair and serious consideration will realize that the responsibility to work for change cannot be denied. It is our fervent hope that this publication will provide some of the inspiration necessary to speed the effort.

The Stephens symposium was an intense intellectual experience that touched the hearts as well as the minds of participants. Those of us who have labored to prepare this report of the proceedings have felt once again, months later, the powerful effect of extraordinary minds focused on the work at hand. Stephens College and the James Madison Wood Research Institute for the Study of Women's Education publish *All of Us Are Present* as a contribution to raising the consciousness of others who share the responsibility of educating women for full participation in the society of the future. We trust that those who read this volume will share our commitment to this vital effort.

Appendix I: Workshops

Twice during the symposium the participants convened in small workshop groups to react to the speeches and panel discussions and raise questions and problems they confronted in their own settings. Each workshop group was led by a three-member team of Stephens faculty and students, one of whom served as a recorder for the session. The following are summaries of issues raised during these workshop sessions, taken from the notes of the recorders.

Special needs of women:

The word which best characterizes these discussions is "choice." Picking up on Patricia Graham's description of today's young woman as "ambivalent," participants noted that educators need to be aware of the array of choices which bewilders the woman student and provides her with the sense of self-worth and power she must have to exercise free choice rather than drift into life situations. Two questions were raised frequently. One concerned the nature of the "power" women students should acquire: what is the proper balance between learning the rules of a male-dominated world and developing a strong sense of oneself as a woman? The other question addressed access to education: how can institutions create more possibilities for poor and third-world women to benefit from education which grants them more choices?

Societal effect and feminist consciousness:

Much discussion concerned the extent of a feminist consciousness among today's college generation. Although educators in women's studies programs and at women's colleges may assume a higher degree of feminist commitment now than in the past, students reported that their peers mistakenly think that all the battles have been won, and some suggested that a true feminist consciousness arises out of frustration at not attaining one's goals rather than out of confidence in one's abilities. A second theme in these discussions was the fear that governmental attitudes and policies were eroding the ground gained in the 1960s and 1970s, and a third was the need to help women students capitalize on their typical means of dealing with problems—networks, mutual

Eleanor Bender, Conference Manager, talks with Louise Quayle, an assistant workshop chair.

support—so that they can change corporate and governmental practices.

Curriculum

Workshop participants expressed concern that as curriculum changes are made, through the incorporation of information about women and the values that are important to them, we do not lose sight of what is good about the traditional curriculum. Otherwise, when one group changes its position in society, a different group becomes oppressed. Some doubt was expressed about the advisability of combining the "old" with the "new" in curriculum building; perhaps it is best to begin at the beginning, making sure that the right elements are incorporated. Attention must be paid to curriculum work at the elementary-secondary levels and at the graduate and adult learner levels. The right kind of planning is inclusive of men and third-world issues. It was suggested that contemporary literature is a rich source of materials which validate the experiences of female students. Students should be active participants in the feminist transformation of the curriculum; planned experiences which link them personally to the subject matter are important, as is learning to make their thinking public. Computer usage is critical for women, for the development of conceptual and communicative skills and the recording and transmission of information.

Agents of Change

Change takes place on several levels, through various types of interactions. Women do not always recognize the power they exercise as change agents; women's education should include advocacy programs which help women to gain practical knowledge of the use of power as diverse individuals who can also work through coalition building. College women who become empowered must also be prepared for post-college experiences which may set them back temporarily. Networks and coalitions can provide a coping mechanism. One of the workshop groups developed a set of resolutions for educational institutions: (1) to encourage the candidacy of persons who openly support the ERA; (2) to endorse the mainstreaming of women and women's history into the curriculum; (3) to endorse the mainstreaming of women, women's history and women's issues in all forms of media; and (4) to resolve that all colleges and universities deliberately create model environments through critical examination of their own institutions.

Bobbie Burk and Nancy Walker

Workshop Leaders

Stephens Faculty:

Jeanine Elliott; Jo Ladwig; Markita Price; Nikki Krawitz; Bennie Ruth Gilbert; Richard Caram; Jean Hamilton; Margaret Campbell; Marilyn White; Connie Beachler; Doris Littrell; Don Scruggs; Kathy Reese; Jane Ellen Ashley; Charles Stuth; Judith Clark; Richard Gelwick; Anne Toland; Barbara Losty; Margie Wade.

Stephens Students

Linda Orlansky; Cindy Donley; Teri Ciacchi; Karen Cutliff; Lee Murphy; Sarah Jaslow; Traci La Rose; Roxanne Rzewnicki; Louise Quayle; Katrina Hegener.

Appendix II: The Speakers and the Panelists

Main Speakers

Patricia Albjerg Graham is dean of the Harvard Graduate School of Education and Charles Warren Professor of History of Education. She served as director of the National Institute of Education from 1977 to 1979. She has written *Progressive Education: From Arcady to Academe* (1967), *Community and Class in American Education* (1974), and coedited with W. Todd Furness *Women in Higher Education*. Her many articles have been published in such journals as *Science*, *Signs*, and *Daedalus*.

Gerda Lerner, a founder in the study of Women's History, is the Robinson-Edwards Professor of History at the University of Wisconsin-Madison. She arrived in the United States in 1939, an Austrian refugee from Hitler. She worked as waitress, secretary, salesgirl, and housewife while gaining competency to write in English. After her two children reached adolescence, she earned her B.A. from the New School for Social Research in New York. By 1966, she had earned her Ph.D. from Columbia University. Her books include *The Grimké Sisters from South Carolina* (1967), *The Woman in American History* (1971), *The Majority Finds Its Past* (1979), and *Teaching Women's History* (1981). She has written a screenplay for *Black Like Me* (1964) and an autobiographical account of her marriage and her husband's death from cancer, *A Death of One's Own* (1978).

Patricia Bell Scott is assistant equal opportunity officer at the Massachusetts Institute of Technology. She has served as director of the Black Women's Education Policy and Research Network and codirector of the Minority Women's Leadership and Development Program, Wellesley College Center for Research on Women. She has written two books and more than twenty of her articles have been published.

Elizabeth Kamarck Minnich is a philosopher and educator. She has served as director of continuing education at Sarah Lawrence College and at Hollins College as well as associate dean of the faculty and assistant to the president at Barnard College. Her recent publications include "A Feminist Critique of the Liberal Arts," in *Liberal Education and the New Scholarship on Women: Issues and Constraints in Institutional Change*, a report of the Wingspread

Conference, the Association of American Colleges, 1982; "Politics and 'Nature,'" in *Comment* (1982); and "Liberal Arts and Civic Arts: Education for 'The Free Man'?" *Liberal Learning* (1983).

Bernice Resnick Sandler is currently an executive associate with the Association of American Colleges, where she has been director of the Project on the Status and Education of Women since 1971. She has also served as deputy director of the Women's Action Program at HEW. She has been associated with women's rights legislation and an education specialist for the U.S. House of Representatives and has played an active role in the passage and implementation of Title IX legislation.

Panelists

Helen S. Astin is professor of higher education at the University of California, Los Angeles. She is also vice-president of the Higher Education Institute. Among her books are *The Woman Doctorate in America, Human Resources and Higher Education* (with Folger and Bayer), and *Some Action of Her Own: The Adult Woman and Higher Education*.

Fontaine Maury Belford is dean and professor of English at Sweet Briar College. She has published articles in such journals as *Maryland Humanities, Soundings,* and the *Journal of Aesthetics,* as well as chapters in two books, *American Utopias: The American Experience,* edited by O. Kraushaar and C. Moment (1980), and *The Compassionate Society,* edited by John M. Richardson, Jr. (1981).

Alison Bernstein is program officer of Education and Culture Programs, United States and International Affairs Programs, at the Ford Foundation. She received her Ph.D. in history from Columbia University in 1983.

William H. Chafe is professor of history at Duke University and codirector of the center of the study of Civil Rights and Race Relations. He is the author of several books, including *The American Woman: Her Changing Social, Political, and Economic Roles, 1920–1970* (1972) and *Women and Equality: Changing Patterns in American Culture* (1977). He received the Robert F. Kennedy Book Award for *Civilities and Civil Rights: Greensboro, North Carolina, and the Black Struggle for Freedom* (1980).

Carolyn Dorsey is coordinator of Black Studies and associate professor of higher education at the University of Missouri-Columbia. She has also worked in the black studies programs at New York University and Indiana State University.

Frances "Sissy" Farenthold is an attorney in Houston, Texas. She is nationally known for her work in women's education. She served for two years in the Texas House of Representatives and is a founder of the National Women's Political Caucus.

Jo Hartley is the founder, editor, and publisher of *Comment*, which focuses on conferences and research about women. She has been a fellow at the Bunting Institute in Cambridge, Mass., a colleague of the Office of Women in Higher Education in Washington, D.C., and an affiliated scholar of the Program for the Study of Women and Men in Society at the University of Southern California.

Eva M. Hooker is associate dean of faculty at Saint Mary's College, where she has taught since 1976. She received her Ph.D. from the State University of New York at Buffalo in 1976.

Arthur Levine is president of Bradford College. He has served as senior fellow at the Carnegie Foundations for the Advancement of Teaching in Washington, D.C. Among his six books is *When Dreams and Heroes Died: A Portrait of Today's College Students*. He has also written numerous articles.

Cynthia Secor is currently the Director of HERS, Mid-Atlantic, where she has been since 1975. Prior to that time, she was a faculty member in the Department of English at the University of Pennsylvania. She is the Co-Director of the Summer Institute for Women in Higher Education Administration, which is held at Bryn Mawr College each year.

Gloria Dean Randle Scott is vice-president of Clark College. She has participated in numerous panels and symposia concerning women's education during her long career as educator and administrator.

Sheila Tobias is coauthor of *What Kinds of Guns are They Buying for Your Butter: A Beginner's Guide to Defense, Weaponry, and Military Spending*, with Shelah Leader, Stefan Leader, and Peter Goudinoff (1982). She is probably best known for *Overcoming Math Anxiety* (Houghton Mifflin, 1980). She is professor of political science at the University of Arizona.

Judith Touchton is associate director of the Office of Women in Higher Education of the American Council on Education in Washington, D.C. She travels widely to speak to and consult with state-based planning groups and panels and to participate in professional development seminars for women.

Appendix III:
Symposium Planning Committee

Bobbie Burk and Nancy Walker, Co-Chairs; Eleanor Bender, Conference Manager; Karen Clough, Assistant Conference Manager; Jeanine Elliott; Dell Keepers; Martha Mumma; Linda Orlansky; Sally Stephenson; Bernice Williamson; Catherine Scroggs.

National Advisory Committee

Carolyn Dorsey; Frances "Sissy" Farenthold; Cynthia Secor; Catharine Stimpson; M. Elizabeth Tidball; Sheila Tobias.

Appendix IV: Participants

Kathleen M. Asher, C.S. Mott Community College
Madolyn Y. Babcock, Stephens Alumna, Stephens Board of Curators
Amanda L. Babin, Stephens SLPS
Barbara J. Bank, University of Missouri, Columbia
Nancy "Rusty" Barcelo, The University of Iowa
Patricia Bennett, University of Missouri, Columbia
Sue Ott-Bennett, Webster College
James Bernhardt, Gustavus Adolphus College
Susan Borwick, Wake Forest University
Rev. Carol Bowers, Saint Paul School of Theology
Richard C. Bowers, University of Maine at Orono
Billie Brandon, Northern Kentucky University
Laura Brewer, Smith College
Mary Nell Bruce, Stephens SLPS
Mary A. Bruemmer, Saint Louis University
Elizabeth Burr, Smith College
Ayse Carden, Agnes Scott College
Anne Carman, University of Missouri, Columbia
Barbara Carter, O'Fallon, Ill.
Ann C. Carver, University of North Carolina at Charlotte
Ann K. Clark, St. Mary's College
Margaret Collison, JMW Institute Board
Nancy Cotton, Wake Forest University
William A. Coulter, Randolph-Macon Woman's College
Gerelee Cunningham, Stephens SLPS
Linda Dagley, University of Missouri, Columbia
Patricia Dean, Gustavus Adolphus College
Mary Dennehy, Tulsa, Okla.
Lisa Dennis, Carlow College-Student
Mary Lynn DeShazo, Sam Houston State University
Rita Deutsch, University of Miami
Victoria Dimidjian, Carlow College

Sister M. Kenan Dulzer, OSU, Ursuline College
Lucille Engelman, Stephens SLPS
Jean Erdman, University of Missouri, Kansas City
Wendy W. Fairey, Barnard College
Sister Kathleen Feeley, S.S.N.D., College of Notre Dame of Md.
Elizabeth Finkbeiner, University of Kansas
Peggy Fitch, Beltsville, Md.
Ida Fleming, O'Fallon, Illinois
Nancy L. Fogarty, Creighton University
Debra Foster, University of Missouri, Columbia
Natalie R. Frager, Germantown, Tennessee
Sister James Francis, OSU, Ursuline College
Jan Friedel, Scott Community College
Pat Gallagher, St. Teresa's Academy
Lisa Gerick, University of Missouri, Columbia
Barbara Gibbs, Texas Lutheran College
Sammye C. Greer, Converse College
Jo Grove, Stephens SLPS
Dorothy A. Haecker, University of Missouri, Columbia
Rose Hagan, Mary Institute
Deborah Haimo, Radcliffe College
Evelyn Haller, Doane College
Jan Harrington, Fiscal Affairs & Data Services, Jefferson City, Mo.
E. Claire Healey, Upper Montclair, N.J.
Darola Hockley, University of Missouri, Columbia
Mary Hoferek, University of Missouri, Columbia
Arlene Horner, Mary Institute
Gué P. Hudson, Agnes Scott College
Jacqueline Hultquist, Central Missouri State University
Jean Isherwood, Stephens SLPS
Pat Jackson, Stephens SLPS
Betsy Jameson, Loretto Heights College
Elizabeth I. Kalau, Coordinator of Elderly Services, Independence, Mo.
Annette Khulmann, Kansas State University
JoAnn Kimball, Doane College
Katherine E. Kleeman, Rutgers University
Kay Klinkenborg, Stephens SLPS
Sharon Lambert, Converse College

Elizabeth Langland, Converse College
Mildred H. Lavin, The University of Iowa
Naomi Linnell, College and University Services, The American Lutheran Church
Betty Littleton, Washington University
La Dona Livingston, Stephens SLPS
Katherine Loring, Great Lakes Colleges Association
Sarah Luthens, University of Missouri, Columbia
Susan McClanahan, The University of Michigan
Susan Coultrap-McQuin, University of Minnesota-Duluth
Jean Steven McVicker, President, Stephens College Alumnae Association
Teresa Massa, Pittsburgh State University
Catherine Mauer, Stephens SLPS
Paula Hooper Mayhew, Bryn Mawr College
Annabel Menchaca, Texas Lutheran College
Betsy Metzger, Sarah Lawrence
Barbara Miller, Stephens SLPS
Nancy K. Miller, Barnard College
Carolyn Moody, Stephens SLPS
Pat Mora, University of Texas at El Paso
Linda Nolan, Stephens SLPS
Mary Lew O'Neill, St. Louis, Mo., Stephens Alumna
Margaret Peirce, C.S. Mott Community College
Deborah J. Pursifull, University of Missouri, Columbia
Pat Ralston, University of Denver
Rosemary W. Reeves, Stephens Alumna, Stephens Board of Curators
Pam Reich, University of Missouri
Sister Mary Marthe Reinhard, SND, Notre Dame College
Frederick F. Ritsch, Converse College
Jean Clinton Roeschlaub, Los Angeles, Calif., Stephens Alumna, Chair, Stephens Board of Curators
Lillian Rose, Covington, Louisiana
Sheila Ruth, Southern Illinois University
Nancy J. Schuessler, Clayton, Mo.
Marcia Schweiss, Stephens SLPS
Jan R. Simon, Pioneer Community College
Karen Small, University of Missouri, Columbia
Margaret Supplee Smith, Wake Forest University

Jamieson Spencer, Mary Institute
Mary White Stewart, University of Missouri, Kansas City
Susan Strom, University of Missouri, Columbia
Ardys A. Thayer, Carlsbad, Calif.
Blanche M. Touhill, University of Missouri, St. Louis
Sandy Underwood, Stephens SLPS
Judy Utz, Missouri Western State College
Judy Vickrey, University of Missouri, Columbia
Carla Waal, University of Missouri, Columbia
Carole O'Brien Walega, Arlington, Va., Stephens Alumnae Association Board Member
Jean M. Ward, Lewis and Clark College
Jodi Wetzel, University of Denver
Bobbe Wheelock, Stephens SLPS
Judith S. White, University of North Carolina at Greensboro
Frances Jones Wilson, University of Missouri, Columbia
Sandy Womack, University of Denver

Bibliography

compiled by Joanna Todd

Abel, Elizabeth, Hirsch, Marianne, and Elizabeth Langland, eds. *The Voyage In: Fictions of Female Development*. Hanover, N.H.: University Press of New England, 1983.

Alcott, Louisa May. *Work: A Story of Experience*. 1892; rpt. New York: Schocken Books, 1977.

Atwood, Margaret. *Surfacing*. New York: Simon & Schuster, 1972.

Barth, John. *Lost in the Funhouse: Fiction for Print, Tape, Live Voice*. Garden City, N.Y.: Doubleday, 1968.

Barthes, Roland, *A Lover's Discourse: Fragments*. New York: Hill & Wang, 1979.

Cantor, Milton, and Bruce Laurie, eds. *Class, Sex, and the Woman Worker*. Westport, Conn.: Greenwood Press, 1977.

Coetzee, J.M. *In the Heart of the Country*. New York: Penguin, 1982.

DuBois, Ellen, ed. *Elizabeth Cady Stanton, Susan B. Anthony, Correspondence, Writings, Speeches*. New York: Schocken Press, 1981.

Eliot, George. *Middlemarch*. New York: Harcourt, Brace & World, 1962.

Fogarty, Nancy. *Shelley in the Twentieth Century: A Study of the Development of Shelley Criticism in England and America, 1916–17*. Atlantic Highlands, N.J.: Humanities Press, 1976.

Frankfort, Roberta. *Collegiate Women: Domesticity and Career in Turn of the Century America*. New York: New York University Press, 1977.

Friedan, Betty. *The Feminine Mystique*. New York: Norton, 1963.

Gennep, Arnold van. *Rites of Passage*. Chicago: University of Chicago Press, 1960.

Gilligan, Carol. *In a Different Voice: Psychological Theory and Women's Development*. Cambridge, Mass.: Harvard University Press, 1982.

Hadewijch. *The Complete Works*. New York: Paulist Press, 1980.

Healey, Claire. "Amy Lowell." *American Women Writers: A Critical Reference Guide from Colonial Times to the Present*. New York: Frederick Ungar, 1979–82.

Herberg, Will. *Protestant, Catholic, Jew*. Garden City, N.Y.: Doubleday, 1956.

Hofstadter, Douglas. *Gödel, Escher, Bach: An Eternal Golden Braid*. New York, Basic Books, 1979.

Hull, Gloria T., Scott, Patricia Bell, and Barbara Smith, eds. *All the Women Are White, All the Blacks Are Men, But Some of Us Are Brave: Black Women's Studies*. Old Westbury, N.Y.: The Feminist Press, 1982.

Komarovsky, Mirra. *Blue Collar Marriage*. New York: Random House, 1964.

Langland, Elizabeth, and Walter Gove, eds. *A Feminist Perspective in the Academy: The Difference It Makes*. Chicago: University of Chicago Press, 1983.

LeClercq, Jean. *Love of Learning and Desire for God: A Study of Monastic Culture*, 3d ed. Bronx, N.Y.: Fordham University Press, 1982.

Lerner, Gerda, *Bibliography in the History of American Women*. 3d rev. ed. Bronxville, N.Y.: Sarah Lawrence College, 1978.

———, ed. *Black Women in White America: a Documentary History*. New York: Pantheon Books, 1972.

———. "The Challenges of Women's History." In *Liberal Education and the New Scholarship on Women; Issues and Constraints in Institutional Change*. Report of the Wingspread Conference. 22–24 October 1981. Washington, D.C.: Association of American Colleges, 1982, pp. 39–47.

———. *A Death of One's Own*. New York: Harper & Row, 1980.

———. *The Female Experience; an American Documentary*. Indianapolis: Bobbs-Merrill, 1977.

———. *The Majority Finds Its Past; Placing Women in History*. New York: Oxford University Press, 1979.

———. *Teaching Women's History*. Washington, D.C.: American Historical Association, 1981.

———. *The Woman in American History*. Menlo Park, Calif.: Addison-Wesley, 1971.

Lightfoot, Sara L. *Worlds Apart: Relationships between Families and Schools*. New York: Basic Books, 1978.

Lundberg, Ferdinand, and Marynia L. Foot Farnham. *Modern Woman: the Lost Sex*. New York: Grosset and Dunlap, 1947.

Millett, Kate. *Sexual Politics*. Garden City, N.Y.: Doubleday, 1970.

Milner, Marion Blackett. *On Not Being Able to Paint*. 2d ed. New York: International Universities Press, 1967.

Moraga, Cherrie, and Gloria Anzaldua, eds. *This Bridge Called My Back: Writings by Radical Women of Color*. Watertown, Mass.: Persephone Press, 1981.

Morrison, Toni. *The Bluest Eye*. New York: Holt, Rinehart and Winston, 1970.

Naisbitt, John. *Megatrends: Ten New Directions Transforming Our Lives*. New York: Warner Books, 1982.

Noble, Jeanne L. *Beautiful, Also, Are the Souls of My Black Sisters: A History of the Black Woman in America*. Englewood Cliffs, N.J.: Prentice-Hall, 1978.

Palmieri, Patricia Ann. "In Adamless Eden: A Special Portrait of the Academic Community at Wellesley College 1875–1920." Ph.D. Diss., Harvard Graduate School of Education, 1981.

Rich, Adrienne. *Snapshots of a Daughter-in-Law: Poems, 1954–1962*. New York: W.W. Norton, 1967.

Ruth, Sheila. *Issues in Feminism: A First Course in Women's Studies*. Boston: Houghton Mifflin, 1980.

Schaef, Anne Wilson. *Women's Reality: An Emerging Female System in the White Male Society*. Minneapolis: Winston Press, 1981.

Scott, M. Gladys, and Mary J. Hoferek, eds. *Women as Leaders in Physical Education and Sports*. Iowa City: University of Iowa Press, 1979.

Shange, Ntozake. *Nappy Edges*. New York: St. Martin's Press, 1978.

Talbot, Marion, and Lois Kimball Rosenberry. *The History of the American Association of University Women, 1881–1931*. Boston: Houghton-Mifflin, 1931).

Tobias, Sheila. *Overcoming Math Anxiety*. New York: W.W. Norton, 1978.

———. *What Kinds of Guns Are They Buying for Your Butter? A Beginner's Guide to Defense, Weaponry and Military Spending*. New York: William Morrow, 1982.

Whitehead, Alfred North. *Aims of Education and Other Essays*. New York: Macmillan, 1929.

Zuckerman, Diana M. "Self-Concept, Family Background, and Personal Traits Which Predict the Life Goals and Sex-Role Attitudes of Technical College and University Women." Ph.D. Diss., Ohio State University, 1977.

Periodicals

Antler, Joyce. "'After College What?': New Graduates and the Family Claim." *American Quarterly* 32 (1980), 409–34.

Baker, Thomas Nelson. "Ideals." *Alexander's Magazine* 2: 5 (1906), 23–29.

———. "Ideals." *Alexander's Magazine* 2: 6 (1906), 37–42.

Graham, Patricia Albjerg. "Expansion and Exclusion: A History of Women in American Higher Education." *Signs: Journal of Women in Culture and Society* 3 (1978): 766.

Jameson, Elizabeth. "To Be All Human: Sex Role and Transcendence in Margaret Fuller's Life and Thought." *University of Michigan Papers in Women's Studies* 1: 1 (1974), 91–126.

Kelly, Joan. "Early Feminist Theory and the 'Querelle des Femmes,' 1400–1789." *Signs* 8 (1982), 4–28.

Lerner, Gerda. "The Necessity of History and the Professional Historian." *The Journal of American History* 69 (1982), 7–20.

Smith, Jonathan Z. "The Bare Facts of Ritual." *History of Religions*, 20 (1980), 112–27.

Welter, Barbara. "The Cult of True Womanhood, 1820–1860." *American Quarterly* 13 (1966): 151–74.

Index

Addams, Jane, 15
Alcott, Louisa May, *Work*, 46
Anthony, Susan B., "Homes of Single Women," 47
Arendt, Hannah, 6, 71–72, 81, 82
Astell, Mary, 38–40

Biblical tradition and interpretation, role of women in, 38–39, 92, 98. See also Astell, Mary; Grimké, Sarah; Mott, Lucretia; Speght, Rachel; Stanton, Elizabeth Cady

Catt, Carrie Chapman, 46
"Cent-Societies," 40–41
Child-care facilities, in relation to women's employment, 31
Civil rights legislation, 21–22. See also National Female Antislavery Conventions
Crummell, Alexander, on the education of black girls (1891), 57. See also Ethnicity
Curriculum, as agent for change, 81–85, 87–89, 100–102, 109. See also Women's Studies

DuBois, W. E. B., and double consciousness, 80

Education, dominant tradition in, defined, 73–75, 84, 87, 96–99; role models in, 94–95, 105–8
Emma Willard's Seminary, 42
Ethnicity, effect of on women's opportunities, 4, 60–70; description of, 55–57. See also Crummell, Alexander; Lightfoot, Sarah; Noble, Jeanne; Rushin, Donna Kate; Shange, Ntozake; Wong, Nellie
Feminism, a definition of, 33–34
Friedan, Betty, *The Feminine Mystique*, 22

Graduate school, effect of on women, 19–20
Grimké, Sarah, *Letters on the Equality of the Sexes*, 39, 44

Lightfoot, Sarah, 61–62. See also Ethnicity
Lyon, Mary, and "cent-societies," 40

Millett, Kate, *Sexual Politics*, 23
Moral Reform Societies, 41–42, 43
Mott, Lucretia, *The Woman's Bible*, 39

National Coalition for Women and Girls in Education, 113
National Female Antislavery Convention, 43–44. See also Civil rights legislation
Noble, Jeanne, on education of black women, 57–58. See also Ethnicity
Nurturant role, 52–53, 81, 89
Palmieri, Patricia, "On Adamless Eden," 14
Pisan, Christine de, 37
"Post-feminist generation," 52
Project on the Status and the Education of Women, 100

141

Querelles de Femmes, 37

Rushin, Donna Kate, "The Bridge Poem," 64–65. *See also* Ethnicity

Shange, Ntozake, *Nappy Edges*, 61. *See also* Ethnicity

Speght, Rachel, *A Mouzell for Melastomus, The Cynicall Bayter and foule mouthed Barker against Evah's Sex*, 38

Stanton, Elizabeth Cady, 39, 44, 45

Stone, Lucy, and "cent-societies," 40–41, 45

Suffrage, women's, 5, 97–98

Swetnam, Joseph, *The Arraignment of Lewd, Idle, Forward and Unconstant Women*, 38

Thomas, M. Carey, 15

Traditional careers for women, 59, 68

Welter, Barbara, "The Cult of True Womanhood, 1820–1860," 11–12

Wingspread conferences: 1972, 7; 1981, 7

Wollstonecraft, Mary, *A Vindication of the Rights of Women*, 11–12

Women's Studies, 35–36, 48, 49, 83, 121. *See also* Curriculum

Wong, Nellie, "When I was Growing Up," 60–61

World War II: effect of on the status of women, 15–18